Lena Horne

With my very best wishes
Charlie Chaplin

Sincerely yours,
Harry Truman

Sophie Tucker

Howard Hughes

John Barrymore

Sincerely yours
Lionel Barrymore

Dale Carnegie

BELIEVE IT or NOT
Ripley

Marion Davies

JAMES MONTGOMERY FLAGG

Moss Hart

Pola Negri

Ronald Colman

LENA HORNE
CHARLIE CHAPLIN
HARRY TRUMAN
LIONEL BARRYMORE
RIPLEY
MOSS HART

LILY PONS
SOPHIE TUCKER
HOWARD HUGHES
JOHN BARRYMORE
DALE CARNEGIE
MARION DAVIES
JAMES MONTGOMERY FLAGG
POLA NEGRI
RONALD COLEMAN

# *Are The Stars Out Tonight?*

*the story of the famous*

## *Ambassador and Cocoanut Grove*

*"Hollywood's Hotel"*

*Margaret Tante Burk*

ROUND TABLE WEST

*Los Angeles, California*

*DEDICATION*

*To all of you out there who have lived, loved and laughed...at the Ambassador. And to all my family around here who have lived, loved and done very little laughing while I have been bound to this shooting star.*



Printed in the United States of America
First Edition

ISBN number 0-937806-00-5

ROUND TABLE WEST
AMBASSADOR HOTEL
3400 Wilshire Boulevard
Los Angeles, California 90010
(213) 387-7011

# INTRODUCTION

Two points I want to make. The first, the story of the great Ambassador Hotel had to be told. For it was and is a vital cog, a veritable chronological moving part and motivation in the wheels of Los Angeles and Hollywood, then and now. A Los Angeles that keeps exploding with its newness and uniqueness, and a Hollywood that is legend second only to Camelot itself...a kingdom like Oz, a glory such as Greece, and a grandeur not unlike Rome.

And in the Ambassador that is home to both, this dazzling past, the hotel's famous and beauteous people's astonishing stories had never been recorded for posterity. Would that I could have had this warehouse of plots when I was penning stories for films and magazines. It's safe to say that millions of features, articles and columns have been written but no real honest-to god book. Dramatic and historical data yes, but so voluminous with its thousands of characters and events, that no one dared tackle it until she came face to face, ear to ear and eye to eye with it.

She? That's the second point.

Every once in a while you see somebody and think "Ah, there's somebody I'd like to meet!"

And not often, but once in a while you meet that person and say to yourself, "Now, this is someone I'd like to know better!"

And then every day, month or year you are glad you met her and richly delighted as you know her better.

Having set that all down, then comes to me first of anybody, very clearly the name Margaret Burk.

Of course, obviously since Mrs. Burk is the famed and coast to coast and border to border popular public relations executive, including in her portfolio the great and unequalled Ambassador Hotel, she has known and been loved by and leaned on by all the famous stars of every walk of life who have lived for five minutes or five years at the Ambassador.

I want to put this down very carefully and clearly...

I have never known any woman so truly kind and so utterly without self-aggrandizement in my life. She is always thinking about you...about your needs or want...never about herself.

Because of these rare qualities she has been confided in...talked to...sought out...by all the greats that pass through this internationally loved hotel...and I should say with the greatest guest list of any hotel in America.

Her mind being both dramatic and sensitive she has been told and remembered tales only she has heard.

How she manages to be top in her field and retain such dignity...I don't know. But she does. And it is we who are hoping she will enjoy and keep us under her wing. She has aided the Ambassador in becoming one of the really rare places.

As a journalist friend of mine Jane Gilman wrote, "The six most valuable words in many an Angelino's vocabulary are: 'I'm a friend of Margaret Burk's.' These may lead you into an interview on a television show, a recording contract, an art exhibit, a meeting with a celebrity or main attraction of an event that attracts thousands.

"She thrives on challenge and hospitality, and when the phone rings in her plaque and trophy decorated office at the Ambassador, she is ready to help...whether business or no."

You see what kind of a person I'm telling you about? And the natural outcome of the two coming together was "Are the Stars Out Tonight." You'll be titillated reading about the famous elegant hotel in the very middle of the picture industry all these years. But also about the Social Elite and the Literary Lions and the Financial Fraternity who are her friends seeking both her advice and company. I know I have.

Gosh, I'm glad I know her! And can sign myself her loving and admiring

Friend,
Adela Rogers St. Johns

# PROLOGUE

*It was Los Angeles' first grand hotel, and it set a precedent for the entire West to emulate. It was located on the pastoral edge of town where guests and the movie colony could enjoy the miles-distant view of hyacinth blue ocean and the gold of the setting sun as they dined in distinguished and elegant surroundings.*

*One afternoon their serenity was interrupted by a gunshot which exploded through the great dining room window and found its target in the arm of one of the diners. The same room where decades later a bullet would fatally pierce the head of a political leader, which is part of the hotel's story.*

*Security was dispatched to apprehend the earlier culprit, and although bandidos were still invading the area, the man carrying the gun was dismissed as a careless hunter who had been shooting rabbits in the adjoining fields. The fields where the skyscraping IBM, Tishman/Prudential and Equitable Buildings now pierce the heavens. And it wasn't all that long ago.*

*The Ambassador's saga reflects that of changing times, of Los Angeles' growth and expansion...her highs and lows and the good and the bad. While dispatching a hotel's vital and traditional services, the Ambassador has contributed to the continuity of the city's development, aided in thrilling career and business dreams becoming reality, and as the standard bearer hotel of the West has made history via its international use and recognition, thereby creating a Los Angeles Window to the World.*

*So theoretically, logically and naturally, someone should write its book. Why me?*

*I guess because its history, experiences and cast of characters intrigued me. Many others, before and after me planned on writing the story, but it was such a gargantuan task spanning so many people and events, that it eluded many, including this writer for a long time. Nonetheless the story...a microcosm and chronological calendar of America's development, the panoramic progression of the entertainment business, Hollywood's legends and excitements and the cross section of business, society, civic, governmental, ethnic and political sequences could not be lost to oblivion.*

*Sad, but true, most of the hotel's records, photos and stories have strayed, been lost or misappropriated (to put it politely) and that's where I came in. Once the book was launched, the army of people who have an affection for the Ambassador emerged to recount stories and memories, and to them I owe much.*

*Now, after hundreds of hours of midnight oil burning, of relentless research, interviews, detective work, monies expended on books and photos, some fruitless excursions into dead-ends and untold technical problems in the twilight zone of self-publishing, I still have the same gripping compulsion to get it in print as I did on day one.*

*Why self-publishing? Because no self-respecting publisher could tolerate the delays which developed when old memories and new material was received and exciting hotel activities still were taking place daily, thus pushing farther and farther ahead the emergence of the book. A paralysis to progress, thus the only solution was to publish "Stars" myself. A cut-off date was hard to determine...*

*She's been a jealous mistress, this hotel, obliquely interrupting personal and professional advancement, financial rewards, leisure time and friendships...most of all the* sweet relationships with my family *who tolerated me and/or my absences while I recreated "Stars" and hers. And I've loved every exasperating minute of it.*

MARGARET TANTE BURK

# TABLE OF CONTENTS

ARRIVALS AND DEPARTURES...EACH DAY BRINGING NEW AND INTERESTING PEOPLE.

The San Francisco Giants waiting for the bus bringing Miss Universe beauty contestants to the hotel. The bus was late...and so were the ballplayers to practice.

The sequestered Manson Jury under heavy guard leaving for Court.

The Muppets arriving for their "Muppets Movie" typical Hollywood Premiere with kleig lights and fans in stands screaming as stars arrived.

Beautiful Joan Crawford greeting Academy Awards banquet in the

Silent screen stars Norma Talmadge to go in his Rolls Royce roadster.

her fans upon her arrival to an
Cocoanut Grove.

and Gilbert Roland deciding where

VIPs frequently arrive by helicopter . . . none more welcome than a smiling Senator John F. Kennedy, . . soon to become U.S. President

Shaun Cassidy.

The Bing Crosby family . . . checking in for a vacation.

# Gloria Swanson: Birthday Girl

Adela, Gloria Swanson's husband Bill Dufty, the birthday girl and Ambassador Executive Chef Marvin Slaughter.

It was just a few months ago, and the inexplicable ghostly consciousness of the steel, stucco and tile-roofed building that has hosted the greats and notables in its bedrooms and on its stages for six decades...could have been mutely joining the actress in reflecting, "Here we are again...coming full circle."

For 6 decades before when the Ambassador Hotel opened in Los Angeles, one of the early-California-Spanish villas was home to Gloria Swanson.

She stood on the stage of the vast, elegant crystal and gold ballroom, this diminutive, glamourous, still exciting actress, widely opening her arms to receive and embrace the wild ovation that was coming to her in waves across the room. She had been everywhere... done everything...and was now back on home ground. Where it had all started.

The applause was tumultuous, the audience was on its feet whistling and cheering. Television cameras were rolling, still cameras clicking, tape recorders absorbing every word, and reporters standing four deep were from Los Angeles, Paris, London, Australia and other far-flung countries of the world. Microphones and note-books were thick on the table in front of the star.

Now living in New York, this was one of Gloria's rare visits to Los Angeles, and biographers, special feature news people, friends and fans that are legion were in attendance to pay homage to her. The beautifully coiffed, gloved and chapeaued "Queen of the Screen"'s popularity hadn't diminished since 1925 when, with her new husband the Marquis de la Falaise, she returned from Europe to be met dockside in New York by 100,000 adoring fans. No less was her triumphant return to Hollywood...thousands of spectators lined the streets from the railroad station to the studio to welcome her.

Gloria, here and now, had reached her 80th birthday, and was celebrating the momentous occasion with her good friend Adela Rogers St. Johns at the Los Angeles' Round Table West literary and celebrity club, which was holding its monthly meeting at the Ambassador.

As young, sassy, brassy, beautiful and talented girls in Hollywood's newly evolving tinsel town, the two were imposing characters in the tapestry of the Ambassador...the home of the stars and of the power-brokers...of the great and the corrupt...the lurid, the passionate...the exalted, the pitied...the Kings and Queens, both royal and phony...of the world.

The great John Barrymore buying flowers for his lady love.

What a group! Bob Hope, John Wayne, Ronald Reagan, Dean Martin and Frank Sinatra. Good friends supporting Reagan's political endeavors at a fundraiser in the Cocoanut Grove.

# Full Circle

"You might say I've come full circle too," said the world's foremost woman journalist Adela Rogers St. Johns later that day, as she looked up from the typewritten pages of her latest novel. Working under a huge umbrella shielding her from the bright California sun, her feet were resting on the original Spanish tiled patio of one of the sand colored adobe bungalows which nestles in the riotously and fragrantly flowered gardens of the Ambassador Hotel grounds.

"I've lived here so many times between my assignments all over the world...for decades past," she reminisced "after the Lindberg baby kidnapping case; after the Windsor's abdication of the throne of England; when Amelia Earhart left for her last fatal flight; when I covered stories under several Presidents; and particularly when I did features for magazines and films...and covered the Hollywood scene.

"This was home for all of us in the early days...a home away from home. The Ambassador was *the* place to live if you had not built your own home. And it was the place to entertain...there was absolutely no other place to go.

"And...almost...there still isn't! The Bella Fontana in the Beverly Wilshire...the Polo Lounge at the Beverly Hills Hotel? *But,* the Ambassador has the history and glamour nobody else can claim.

"Back then, the film stars and producers didn't have the large and beautiful homes they have today... nor did they know how to entertain in the grand, elegant and aristocratic manner that the hotel could provide. So this is where we all came to meet one another, to be seen, to be coddled, amused and entertained. And this is where business, society and the film people met. Formerly film and theatrical people had not been 'accepted' by the social elect...but hotel functions brought them together."

And no little influence did the writer have on the social acceptance of the film element. Daughter of famed criminal lawyer Earl Rogers, her grandfather had brought his family West where his duties as a circuit minister had directed him. Her grandmother became the first woman university professor in the state of California; a pioneer with Phoebe Apperson Hearst to found the PTA; and her musician aunt aided in augmenting art and music as one of the founders of the Hollywood Bowl.

Adela's world encompassed business and society.

"The fabulous costumes, parties and balls were like fairy tales, beautiful and exciting" she continued.

"The Cocoanut Grove was a party every night where the stars provided the entertainment with their talent and enthusiasm. There wasn't an evening when you couldn't find several stars in the audience and on the stage. It was the *in* place. And what fun we had.

"I remember writing about Joan Crawford when I visited the Grove one evening with the town's pet bride and groom, Victoria and Tom Mix. I found myself staring at an unknown girl dancing with the tall dark youth, Mike Cudahy, heir to the Chicago packing fortune. I wrote, 'from her too-high heels to her too-frizzy hair, she was all wrong, yet she stood out as though the light was too bright for anyone but her. Terribly young, showing off rather crudely, laughing too loudly, she had a fierce and wonderful vitality and grace. Lucille Le Sueur (as was her real name) has done a few bits at MGM. I think she's on her way.' "

Crawford remembered it too. "My skirts had to be a trifle shorter, my heels a little higher, my hair a tint brighter and my dancing faster. One night during a Charleston contest, I lost a slipper dancing with Jack Ensley at the Grove. We didn't stop to retrieve it, and the crowd applauded...and of course, we won another trophy.

"The 'hotcha kid' I was called, the 'hey-hey girl', and those terms embarrassed me even then, but the only time I felt I belonged was when I was on the dance floor. It was worth it. The newspapers exploited my 'new beau every night', and the fact that I had 'more cups than the Brown Derby'! And Hollywood saw me in action... which was all-important to a fledgling actress. Not only did I love dancing, I worked hard at it, and I won over 100 trophies. My zeal for living, dancing and excitement didn't go unnoticed by producers. It was the reason for my getting the lead in my first big picture, OUR DANCING DAUGHTERS!

"There was so much drama right here in this hotel...so many lives were affected, some for better, some for worse. So many careers began...some even ended in this very room," said the famous actress who had learned all the ropes, all the ups and downs of the film business in her long, perilous, but successful career.

Joan Crawford's big brown eyes traveled around the great nightclub, the Cocoanut Grove where she had spent untold evenings during its more than half-century existence...this evening, to present a Golden Globe Award to her good friend, John Wayne. With intense emotion she said, "What memories I have of this place."

# Hostess to the World

Over 20 million nights of comfort have been offered guests in Ambassador Hotel bedrooms since the light of its first day, January 1, 1921. Some weary from travel and business; some in hot pursuit of pleasure and excitement; some to be entertained or to see how the movie colony lives. Some seeking business and new horizons, some overnighters, many who have sojourned for months or years in the famous bungalows calling the gracious and hospitable atmosphere, *home*.

It is unlikely that there is any other hotel in the world that has cradled quite the *variety* of people; catered to as many renowned and worldly; shown hospitality to intellectuals, celebrities, royalty, film stars, business tycoons; the rich, poor, the famous and infamous; tourists, and local participants; not to mention sultans, sheiks, presidents and politicians...perhaps even a few demimondes...as the Ambassador.

This Grande Dame has been mistress to generations of star crossed lovers, friends, strangers...even enemies. She has entertained, caressed and warmly comforted each of them...while exaltedly singing their praises. Or perhaps discreetly keeping or burying their secrets.

"Going on" sixty, she still is endowed with beauty and wisdom...while exuding the charm and charisma of a girl in her teens. She still relishes the visits of her old friends and aficionados, while daily making new ones of each ensuing generation. She has tendered all manner of affectionate favors to hundreds of thousands of guests in her 21 thousand Arabian Nights career.

This is her story and theirs. And perhaps yours.

To its guests, the Ambassador hasn't been just heaven or haven. As with Hollywood and its early tempestuous days, it has witnessed the gamut of all conditions, robbery, murder, drunkenness, despair, marriage, divorce, illicit affairs, orgies, pranks, fights, suicides, frustration, and mate-swapping.

Fabulously wild and extravagant parties, serious seminars, banquets, grand balls, conferences and conventions...civil, civic and community endeavors, trade shows, promotions, press conferences, political affairs, movie-making, formal Hassidic traditional weddings...some elopements...all have been de rigueur.

Then there are the musicals, name entertainment, award features, beauty contests, society affairs, straight and bizarre functions, bar mitzvahs, all nature of ethnic ceremonies, debuts, sweet sixteen parties, movies shown...premiered...filmed; from diamond anniversaries to parties for the nursery set...which have found their way to this hotel. Some happy, some sad as in the case of the assassination of a popular hero.

**The entrance. Classical lines of the towering pylon soaring over the Fountain of All Nations "was a beacon of progress on the city's finest thoroughfare, Wilshire Boulevard." (And adding a glamorous greeting was a scantily clad statue for which famous film star Betty Grable had posed.)**

Where else in the world would you find doormen greeting presidents and world leaders, chief telephone operators Goldie Palmer and Iris Hill conversing with residents and garnering autographs of Winston Churchill, Madame Galli-Gurci, Howard Hughes, Harold Lloyd, Doris Duke, Maurice Chevalier, Admiral Byrd, Texas Guinan, Charles Chaplin, Charles Lindbergh, Mary Pickford, Jim Garner, Robert Conrad, Robert Stack, Robert Wagner, Angie Dickinson and Ronald Reagan...to name a few of thousands.

Where else could you find residing under the same roof, John Barrymore with his monkey Clementine, Gloria Swanson and her new baby, Charles Chaplin (always romancing several sweethearts at the same time); Marion Davies riding a horse through the lobby to a party to amuse her ever-loving William Randolph Hearst (with whom she shared a wing on the second floor for months at a time); Rudolph Valentino's nocturnal visits to Pola Negri and Norma Talmadge; FBI Chief J. Edgar Hoover and his bodyguards rooming next door to Walter Winchell (busy writing his daily columns); Senior Hughes and his young son Howard...later Noah Dietrich aiding Howard in building a multimillion dollar empire while endeavoring to disentangle his innumerable romantic pecadillos; Sid Grauman's practical jokes aided and abetted by manager Ben Frank, Sid's planning of the "footprints" at his Chinese Theatre; Mack Sennett's discovery of Bing Crosby at the Grove...and Bing's fight to find his fame and sobriety; both Bing and Jack Benny proposing to their to-be wives among the Cocoanuts; Nikita Khrushchev drinking of wife-opposed vodka with newsmen and his ire at being refused Disneyland; famed writer and wit Wilson Mizner holding court; special waitresses who were such favorites that guests willed money and diamonds to them.

Al Jolson, Charlie Chaplin and Joe Penner swimming and diving for the amusement of pretty girls in the Olympic size outdoor pool, pulling off Eddie Cantor's suit so he couldn't get out of the pool until dark.

Bathing beauty Shirley Temple, relaxing between dance rehearsals.

**Stars in residence. Gloria Swanson, Charlie Chaplin and Marion Davies.**

Visualize Pavlova rehearsing her dazzling feet in an empty ballroom which later witnessed Shirley Temple learning her tap steps from "Bo Jangles" Robinson; airplane ace Jacqueline Cochran operating the Ambassador Beauty Shop...before present operator Antonio was born; Jean Harlow dancing and loving William Powell in the Grove...scant months before she married Paul Bern; Bern's visit to an Ambassador bungalow the afternoon of his suicide; Russ Columbo's rise to crooner-fame in the Grove, cut off when an accidental bullet was put through the singer's head by his best friend; an early singing and piano playing career surfacing for Merv Griffin; movies and scripts planned by D.W. Griffith, Elinor Glyn and others. Scott and Zelda Fitzgerald gloriously arriving atop a taxi singing and drinking champagne...then ignominiously leaving the hotel in the dead of night, after piling their suite's furniture in the middle of the parlor with their "unpaid bill" on top and setting fire to it.

Distinguished guests at the "Hollywood Night" dinner dance. Right to left: Kay Francis, Ben Lyon, Joan Bennett, Clark Gable, Louella Parsons, Gary Cooper, Mrs. Clark Gable, Joel McCrea, Mrs. Harold Lloyd, Dr. Harry Martin, Mary Carlisle, William Powell, Gene Markey, Bebe Daniels, Carole Lombard. The following guests are not in the photograph; Douglas Fairbanks, Harold Lloyd, Wallace Beery, John Marsh, Constance Talmage, Lilyan Tashman, Edmund Lowe, Lily Damita, Kenneth McKenna and Mr. and Mrs. James Gleason

**"Hollywood Night" (in the early days when stars took over the Grove stage and entertained themselves)**

**Singer Rouvan...in recent times, with his stage extravaganza.**

Another command performance when all movieland paid homage to gossip columnist Louella Parsons. Woe be to anyone absent!

Joan Crawford finding the Grove "her" place where she won Charleston contests, seductively romanced Clark Gable, and presented John Wayne with a Golden Globe Award, with his bejewelled and elegant wife Pilar watching; a young S.C. football-playing student John Wayne saving his money to go "tea-dancing" at the Grove while courting his first wife Josephine Saenz.

Real contrast to the Warner Records "coming out" party in the seventies for Alice Cooper featuring sound which reached blocks away, songs which included an electric chair and a snake, freakily costumed and exotic people dancing, more frequently boy-boy and girl-girl...crowned only by "Alice" swinging from the elegant, decades old crystal chandeliers, while featuring a black, female 350-pound performer executing a topless dance garbed only in an enormous pantie.

Somewhere in-between there were other thrills and fascinations.

Could anyone who saw her forget young and aspiring model Norma Jean's efforts to learn at the Emmaline Snively Blue Book Modeling Agency in the hotel...her photographic sessions and beauty contest participation? Her attendance at the Cocoanut Grove with her new husband and first orchid corsage...or her wiggly never-to-be forgotten Academy Award appearance as Marilyn Monroe. And innumerable interesting activities with lovers and friends in-between?

How unique to witness Apollo Ten astronauts, fresh from a visit to the moon, "landing" on the hotel lawn for us mere mortals to meet. About that time, we were loaned a moon rock brought back to earth from the Sea of Tranquility by Neil Armstrong to see and touch...from that far-off moon.

They're all still here...some in person, some in phantom or spirit...because the scenes have been too vital and exciting to fade into obliviousness, the cast of characters too potent and colorful to disappear...or perhaps because many of their emulating children and grandchildren are still around.

**Joan Crawford acting in a scene with the "King", Clark Gable. Only they weren't acting. A hot love affair lasted a long time for the popular pair. Note Miss Crawford's see-through blouse,...a not-so-new fashion note.**

Frequent guest...Benny Goodman. The "King" of Swing.

Robert Young and his lovely Betty celebrated their wedding evening in the Ambassador, and return for their anniversaries and other celebrations.

Today's picture is no less colorful.

A bemused Benny Goodman walking down the hall, horn under his arm on the way to but another concert or recording session.

Freddy Martin setting up in the Grove...for a private party.

Handsome movie star turned politico, Ronald Reagan, on the campaign trail aided and abetted by Bob Hope, Dean Martin, John Wayne and Frank Sinatra. *All performing* in the Grove, in the same evening.

"Police Woman", "The Graduate", "Medical Center", "Wonder Woman", "Elvis", "Skag", "Dallas", "Shaun Cassidy" and dozens of other films and television series being shot "on location" at the hotel, and watched by tourists from all over...knowing they're really in Hollywood. Even the Muppets "Miss Piggy" and "Kermit the Frog" had a real Hollywood premiere with "real people" in the audience. All Hollywood was there.

Bejewelled, satin and lace Gay Community participants in their beauty pageant to select their Queen in the Grove;...between superstars Sammy Davis, Liza Minelli, Wayne Newton and dozens of other performer's engagements.

Competitive high school proms playing simultaneously in the ballrooms with the tuxedoed or weirdly dressed boys brawling with each other...as their parents before them did. Then "making out" with their sweetly gowned dates on walks through the vast, shadowy, mimosa and jasmine scented gardens. As their parents before them did.

Do they feel the presence of a John Barrymore tenderly kissing Dolores Costello in the same garden? Or see the reflection of the "It" girl, Clara Bow wildly dancing around the fountain, her only garment wetly clinging to her sexy form for her audience...the University of Southern California football team.

And do the ghosts still carry the sparks that flew between the vast crowd rallying close to their new political hero as he addressed them in those same sweetly-scented, grassy-green open Gardens only one day...a brief moment in time...before he was felled by an assassin's bullet in the yawning chrome and white kitchens of the hotel. Writing still another chapter, a devastating one, in the life of the Ambassador.

If ghosts do live, the handsome Robert Kennedy could have had an even greater audience watching his electrified rally. For the hundreds of eyes...the hotel windows of bungalows and rooms on the garden side have been home to Howard Hughes, Marion Davies, Pola Negri, Walter Winchell, Clark Gable, and Marilyn Monroe...watching with Bobbie's brother John.

Filming of "The Great American Contest", an ABC movie of the week. Barbie Benton, Farrah Fawcett, Kathy Bauman, Susan Damonte, Tracy Reed and Joanna Cameron along with Eleanor Parker and Louis Jourdan filmed at the hotel for three weeks.

**Earlier beauties were the models studying with the hotel's Emmaline Snively Blue Book Modeling Agency.** Emmaline found one potential "Star" working for Reginald Denny Aircraft and offered her free lessons until she could pay for them out of modeling jobs. Can you find Marilyn Monroe?

On location at the Ambassador, "Wonder Woman" Lynda Carter, "Police Woman" Angie Dickinson, and "Pin-Up" Betty Grable.

My love affair with the Ambassador Hotel began before "ever I saw her face". It was in the late thirties when all over America, every Saturday night at parties in our own living rooms we danced to the music of Freddy Martin, Phil Harris, Ozzie Nelson, Rudy Vallee, Hal Kemp, Orrin Tucker, Horace Heidt, and all of the other marvelous bands broadcasting "coast to coast from the world-famous, star-studded Cocoanut Grove in the Ambassador Hotel in Los Angeles". Then the announcer would interview the film stars as they danced by.

It was even more exciting for this music-loving teenager because I was the vocalist with our Austin High School dance band in Chicago. So on the family's first vacationing motor trip to Los Angeles, the ride down Wilshire Boulevard and seeing the keenly anticipated Ambassador for the first time was a momentous occasion in my life.

Nor were we prepared for the casual and relaxed look of the city. A lady dressed in a kimono was watering the lawn of her house which faced the bustling and elegant Wilshire Boulevard which in Chicago, would have called for suit, hat and gloves, then seeing a floral shirted man boarding a bus for work, with gardenias sprouting out of the headband of his hat.

The brilliant unsmogged rays of the sun hitting chalky white and coral colored buildings were sharp contrasts to the dark and dingy Midwestern edifices to which I was accustomed. I remember being relieved to think that movie stars didn't effect dark glasses to be ostentatious or haughty, rather to protect their eyes from the glare.

And so did I don my dark glasses like all other Angelenos and immediately become one.

And what a culture shock after buildings in the East that didn't allow for a sliver of space between them, coming upon the vast green lawns and startlingly beautiful flowers fronting the Ambassador property... the regal and glamourous statue on the tower of the drive-

way for which curvaceous Betty Grable had posed. As we drove through we could see passengers on the loaded double-decker Wilshire bus leaning over from both aisles to see "Betty Grable", too.

What a thrill to read PHIL HARRIS AND HIS ORCHESTRA NOW APPEARING on the famous Grove electric sign...after listening from so many miles away.

Soon the family left for home, allowing my brother (later to be California Superior Judge James Tante) and me to stay on in an apartment near the hotel. Visiting the Ambassador Theatre was all our budget could accommodate, until on Thanksgiving, Mother sent us a $10 check to "have a nice dinner", which we did with *champagne, turkey and all the trimmings* at the Grove.

Dancing to the music of Jan Garber, he leaned over the bandstand to us and remarked that we made a lovely couple...we even looked alike! Before we had time to explain, he was smiling and talking to the couple dancing next to us. Howard Hughes, with Ginger Rogers nestled in his arms.

Soon Chicago and college beckoned, so back I went, but it was to be only temporary. I was home.

More than four decades later, again Jim and I were dancing together at the Grove on the occasion of the extravagant, star-studded televised premiere of THE MUPPET MOVIE, which now, I, associated with the hotel, had coordinated. And who should dance by, still as resplendent and gorgeous as in all those years before...Ginger Rogers.

Naturally we got to talking about "the good old days" which is an Angeleno pastime...with Liberace, Johnny Mathis, Ethel Merman and others...reminiscing about nostalgic, wonderful times in the hotel and Grove, while enjoying present day ones. An avid audience included "Angel" Cheryl Ladd, Raquel Welch, David Cassidy...many of today's stars enjoying the glamour and excitement that the Grove has always inspired people from all over the world.

During the intervening years, summers would find me vacationing at the Ambassador; war years meant tea dances with uniformed service men on their way out to the Pacific front; later family and friends' social affairs at the hotel; and my first night out after the birth of my first son, again the Grove, of course. Then, much, much later...the wedding reception of that same son Tray and his lovely Marie.

The debutante ball including my daughter Linda, and her young 16 year old brother, Jim, about to squire another deb, admiring his first white tie and tails, in the full length hotel mirror...commenting, "Now if I could only dance."

As with so many Angelenos, the hotel figured heavily in my life and social affairs.

But it was business that associated me with the hotel.

As a vice president of a financial institution headquartered on Wilshire Boulevard, I participated in the business activity of the Wilshire Chamber of Commerce...soon becoming the organization's first lady president. Presiding over meetings and functions at the Ambassador, I also organized other successful business and civic affairs which attracted thousands of business and residential neighbors to the hotel. This did not escape the attention of then manager Hugh Wiley who offered me the job of public relations director. Though perhaps not as serious or prestigious as my former occupation, the possibility offered excitement, meeting important personages and interesting personalities from all over the world...so I was hooked. Now, 10 years, hundreds of events and thousands of people, not to mention many other extraordinary experiences that would challenge even the most vivid of imaginations, later...I must admit, it was a good decision.

"If only," I have mused a million times, "the Ambassador could talk...what a story it would tell." But it can't and I can...so why didn't I do it?

I have, and here it is. I hope you, the reader, enjoy the grand and glorious, sometimes bizarre exploits of the Ambassador as much as I have enjoyed researching, writing and living many of them.

Early Los Angeles Chamber of Commerce brochure promoting the city to attract tourists and settlers "To the land of perfect climate, sunshine and oranges".

# El Pueblo De Nuestra Senora La Reina De Los Angeles De Porciuncula

...THEN AND NOW...

El Pueblo de Nuestra Señora La Reina de Los Angeles de Porciuncula, Los Angeles' proper name, translation: the Town of Our Lady the Queen of the Angels of Porciuncula, was founded in 1781 by 44 somewhat reluctant colonists from Mexico. The town was ordained by royal decree after Felipe de Neve, governor of California, recommended to the Viceroy of Mexico that it was an ideal spot for a mission.

In 1822, Mexico won her independence from Spain, and in 1847 Alta California won her independence from Mexico. Twenty-eight years later, California was admitted to the United States. It was 1850.

☆ ☆ ☆ ☆

The pioneers...first of a long line of would-be Angelenos...tramped across the Colorado Desert to stop first at San Gabriel, where they were escorted by the Neve's soldiers to the pueblo site. There was a plaza and town lots were plotted on the ground. It was Los Angeles' first subdivision. The soldiers fired a salute with their flintlock carbines, and the new settlers formed a procession around the plaza while a San Gabriel padre blessed the lots. De Neve decreed, and the city name came into being. The date was September 4, 1781... six weeks before the American colonies on the other side of the continent assured their independence from England with their victory in Yorktown.

It wasn't too long before Los Angeles was referred to as the predicted capital of the West.

☆ ☆ ☆ ☆

Presently, upwards of 15 million visitors a year are hosted in Los Angeles. The city has become the major business and financial center of the West Coast. New hotels and high-rise office buildings light up the downtown skyline, joining with skyscrapers on Wilshire as the fashionable boulevard rambles all the way down to the sea.

The Ambassador is located in the very heart of the city, midway between Downtown and Beverly Hills, neighboring to Hollywood, and in easy direction to fine shops, theatres and tourist attractions.

Los Angeles offers a pace that is jet-propelled or leisurely, from the World Trade Center, Music Center, ARCO Plaza (the nation's largest subterranean shopping center) all contribute to the vitality and verve that is downtown L.A.... to Hollywood's Walk of Fame and Mann's (nee Grauman's) Chinese Theatre renowned for star's footprints; West Los Angeles (home of UCLA); Santa Monica and up the picturesque coastline to Malibu; busy, bustling Marina Del Rey with its sailboats and discos; suburban San Fernando Valley, home of many movie studios.

Tourist attractions abound. Disneyland, Knott's Berry Farm, Museums, Magic Mountain, Universal Movie Studio Tour, Marineland, Lion Country Safari, Ports O'Call, the Queen Mary, Farmer's Market, the Hollywood and Rose Bowls, L.A. Zoo, the Greek Theatre, the Planetarium, Dodger Stadium, Lawry's Food Center, Huntington Library, Sports Arena, the Forum and Coliseum...and Catalina Island in the blue Pacific is but 45 miles away.

Sports prevail year-round in the moderate climate, with sun and desert, snow and mountains, rivers, lakes and ocean mere minutes away.

Restaurants, settlements and broad ethnic representation provide exotic and international flavor.

And Los Angeles is a mecca for museum, art, theatre and culture devotees.

The little pueblo that is as old as attained American independence; and was 50 years old when Chicago was incorporated, is still considered "the newest city in the world. A city without a past, while as up-to-date as the latest issue of your newspaper."

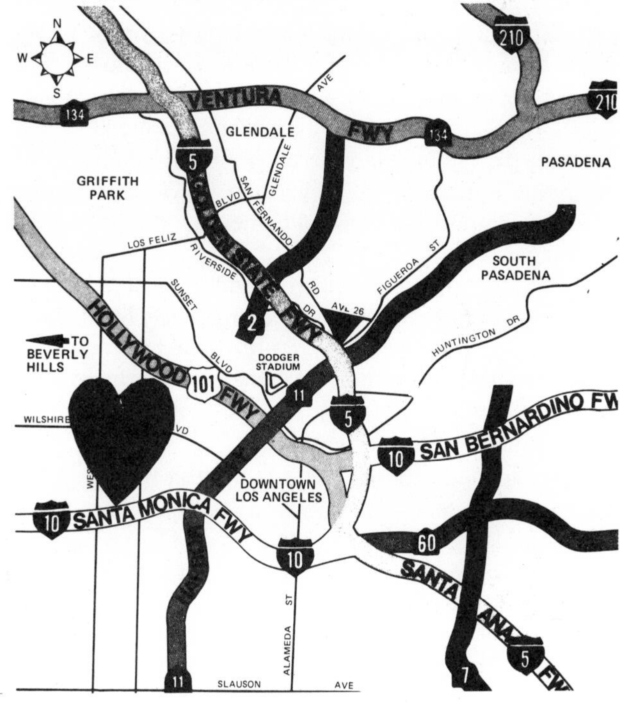


The Ambassador...geographic and affectionate heart of Los Angeles.

# Gottfried Schmidt's Little Dairy Farm

Former home of Reuben Schmidt and his family on Wilshire Boulevard...now the main entrance to the Ambassador.

Much California property found its way into private ownership through Spanish and Mexican colonizations; as vast ranchos granted to individuals at the discretion of the Governor; or as parcels of land designated as pueblos (cities).

The quarter section (160 acres) where the Ambassador Hotel now stands, was part of the parcel "claimed" by Gottfried Schmidt in 1870 by virtue of the Pre-Emption Act which applied to not yet designated or "public" land. Having been enacted in 1841, before California joined the Union in 1850, the act provided settlers the legal right to settle and improve these unappropriated public lands, and later to buy the land at the minimum government purchase price of $1.25 an acre. Early records list Schmidt as a farmer who, with his wife Hulda Franciska and their three sons, lived on the land for 30 years.

"Sparkling clear water coursed down from Silver Lake, became the healthful Bimini Baths, then continued down to around Vermont and Fourth Streets south to Sixth and Catalina...then continued down through the Ambassador area on its way to Playa del Rey. But not all of it," according to George Reaves Schmidt, grandson of the first owner of the property the hotel now rests on.

"My father, Judge Ruben Schmidt, with his father and two brothers dammed up the stream at Wilshire and Mariposa, made a pond, built a bridge over it and used it as their swimming hole. All the neighborhood kids built rafts and caught frogs, where later we were to play around the hotel construction.

"Tules and willows grew along the banks of the stream. Wilshire Boulevard was a swamp, where I as a boy, found fish fossils and Indian relics. Dad used to go to school 'up on the hill', riding his horse to Westlake Park which was then a garbage dump. There he would catch the cable car up to Los Angeles High School east of town. The horse would make his way back to the ranch to do the chores, and Dad would then have to walk back from Westlake after school. He and his brothers carried their slingshots with which they would bag rabbits for their supper."

In 1902, Schmidt sold the portion (23 acres, presently the hotel property) to Ella Crowell, half of which she sold to the Los Angeles Pacific Railway Company for the purpose of constructing an interurban railway. This plan did not develop, so in 1919 both the railway company and Mrs. Crowell sold their halves to the Hotel Company. In June of 1919 ground was broken, and building was started on the estimated $5 million dollar hotel (at that time, an unbelievable amount of money), which had originally been conceived and promoted by enterprising business men and the Los Angeles and Wilshire Chambers of Commerce as a civic endeavor.

The Wilshire area had been considered too far away from the center of things to have much value in 1919. Developers in early Los Angeles, such as William Garland, insisted that "people won't drive home from their day's work facing into the sun, so the city will continue its spread East."

But they were wrong. Angelenos turned around and marched west into the sun all the way down to the sea to become sun-worshipers and dwellers.

And so the Ambassador Hotel was the cause of Wilshire Boulevard becoming the "smart" street...the Fifth Avenue...the main artery of Los Angeles.

Seventh Street had originally been planned to be the main thoroughfare forging west from downtown to handle traffic. The fact is, the hotel was required to be built, in compensation, with foundations and sub-engineering to allow for a subway train which could continue along Seventh. This was the provision of the Pacific Railway Company, thus a network of tunnels still exists under the building. In the early days they were heavily used to transport carts of provisions, foodstuffs and illegal booze to all of the bungalows to which they led. One can contemplate the tunnels' accessibility aiding clandestine folly and romance.

★ ★ ★

The New York Times.

ARMISTICE SIGNED, END OF THE WAR!
BERLIN SEIZED BY REVOLUTIONISTS;
NEW CHANCELLOR BEGS FOR ORDER;
OUSTED KAISER FLEES TO HOLLAND

**Dancing in the Streets** of many American cities greeted the news that the armistice ending the war had been signed.

**DANCING IN THE STREETS. Mary's mother greeting Douglas Fairbanks, Mary Pickford and Charlie Chaplin upon their return home at war's end following their successful bond selling tour. They had raised millions of dollars for the war effort, and were ready to go back to work...making movies.**

# A New Era

The year 1919 was ushered in with a celebration that rivalled Armistice Day. Parades and ceremonies had welcomed soldiers home from the war and gold star flags were still flying about the city for those who would not return.

Los Angeles got a head start on the rest of the nation in resuming "business as usual" because she didn't have as much renovating and retooling to do. Only the shipyards in the state had had any major involvement in the war effort.

It had been a year for fresh beginnings everywhere and Los Angeles and its blossoming movie business had its stars, Mary Pickford, Douglas Fairbanks, Charlie Chaplin and Marie Dressler, as well as others back from the front and from the war bond and money raising efforts, again making pictures.

The "War President" Woodrow Wilson visited Los Angeles and received great ovations. A week later, Wilson, winner of a Nobel Prize, suffered a nervous breakdown never to recover.

War hero General Pershing came to Los Angeles and found a park named after him; royalty was represented with the visit of the King and Queen of Belgium who were greeted by thousands; famous ace Eddie Rickenbacker executed his transcontinental flight in an all-metal monoplane promoting air mail service...and illegal booze surfaced in the wake of laws of Prohibition which went into effect almost simultaneously, though coincidentally, with the visit of President De Valera of the Irish Republic.

Coincidental to the visits of important personages and the increase of adventurous tourists, a group of civic-minded Angelenos encouraged by the principal banking and financial interests of the city, forged ahead with their plans for a hotel to accomodate this anticipated influx of people to the west coast.

Los Angeles Sunday Times

THE ONLY NEWSPAPER ROTOGRAVURE SECTION WEST OF THE ROCKIES

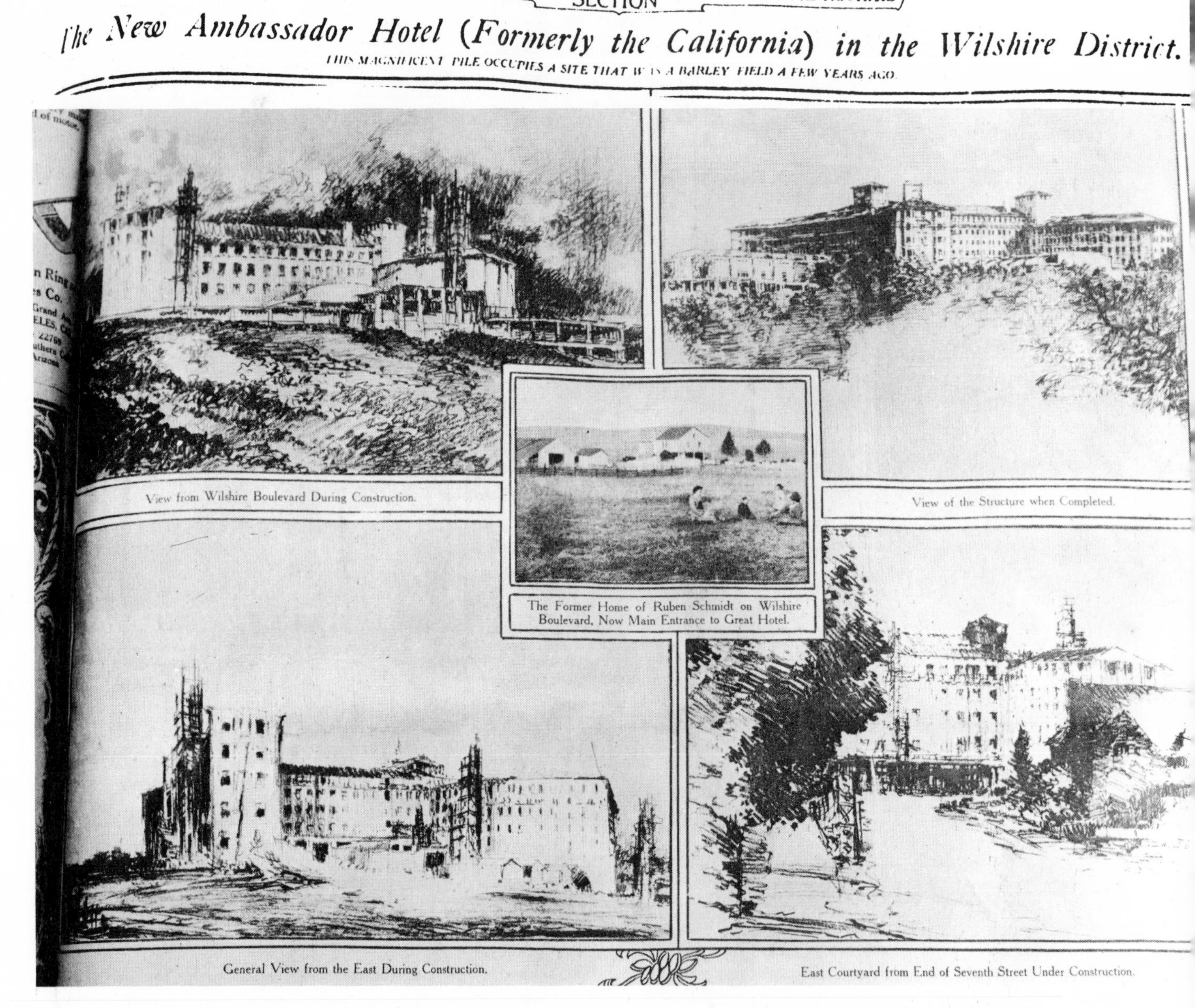
The New Ambassador Hotel (Formerly the California) in the Wilshire District.

THIS MAGNIFICENT PILE OCCUPIES A SITE THAT WAS A BARLEY FIELD A FEW YEARS AGO.

View from Wilshire Boulevard During Construction.

The Former Home of Ruben Schmidt on Wilshire Boulevard, Now Main Entrance to Great Hotel.

View of the Structure when Completed.

General View from the East During Construction.

East Courtyard from End of Seventh Street Under Construction.

# Planning A Grand Hotel

"When a city reaches that point in its development which causes a hotel to rear itself within its limit, then that city can well be said to have 'arrived'," so wrote Joe Minster in his Hotel Magazine. "A city is known by its hotels, so the hospitality of a city can be judged thereby. Thus, the seven league strides of Los Angeles which have been the wonder of the whole country for more than a decade...that 'little wintering place' is today a great metropolis ranked only by the age-old centers of the east.

'To cap such achievements nothing is more fitting than that a great hotel, calculated to arrest national attention, will be established in this city."

In planning the Ambassador, its mentors determined it would be a great and significant hotel, and so of course, they engaged the best professionals to make it become a reality.

Joe Minster predicted it would be the star in the crown of the City of the Angels.

# The Ambassador, the "Jewel in Los Angeles Crown"

"A fittingly located tourist hotel finds itself in the heart of the best residence district of any city, so the Wilshire district was naturally turned to," observed Myron Hunt, architect chosen to design the hotel. "Much to the surprise of even the old-time residents, a park of twenty-two acres in the heart of the area was found on a hilltop unoccupied and available, with a frontage on Wilshire Boulevard of six hundred and sixty feet, and with a depth of more than twice this, carrying the property to Eighth Street and a car line, the hilltop centering upon Seventh Street, the principal district of the city.

"Too costly to grade the hill and fill the valley for residential purposes, the property was ideal for a hotel."

Considered an heroic undertaking "The California" as it was called, was originally conceived and promoted as a civic enterprise. The plan was in danger of being lost and needed outside capital which appeared in the form of S.W. Straus, head of the powerful bonding house bearing his name. Mr. Straus stepped Aladdinlike into the breach and saved the venture. Upon refinancing, the hotel became "The Ambassador", part of the Ambassador Hotels System, which included the Ambassador Hotels in Atlantic City, New York, Santa Barbara, and the Alexandria in Los Angeles.

Officials of the hotel were: Vice President and General Manager Vernon Goodwin; Secretary Treasurer Grover Sholem; Resident Manager William Banks; and Attorney H.W. O'Melveny.

Three essentials, more important than the careful placing of brick and mortar asserted themselves in the planning of the hotel. (1) The visitor should find its accomodations surpassingly good; (2) it should become a social center for both public and private use in which Los Angeles had been lacking; and (3) it should create a civic life of such importance that the people of the community would be proud of its possession.

# In the Beginning

Architect Myron Hunt

Brick and mortar plans were left to Architect Hunt.

"The contour of the property results in the two principal sides (the south and east) fill the top of the hill, while the north side drops off sufficiently to make it possible to have a ballroom on a level with the lobby, with parking space, entrance foyer, shops, and even a theatre on the Casino level...but all above ground and with natural sunlight.

"And from the lobby floor, the surrounding mountains are commanded in every direction, while the deep hollow in the center of the back has resulted in a service department, including all the usual underground burrows of a great hotel, which is completely above ground...completely lighted and having natural ventilation.

"Three things distinguish the hotel proper. First, the H-shaped plan with flaring corners, letting the sunlight into every room; second, the method of planning which provides a window in every bathroom, as well as two windows for every room; and, third, the great feeling of space given by the arrangement of Lobby, Dining Room and Ball Room, so schemed that it is possible to stand on the stage of the Ball Room and see four hundred and fifty feet through the building, or on the terrace in the East Court and look almost that distance across the lobby, through the Dining Room and on toward the Santa Monica Mountains and the sea.

"The panorama from the hilltop is the same that one gets from every hilltop in Los Angeles, with the mountains on two sides, the sea on the west, and the distant reaches of the sea and valley to the south, and over the Palos Verdes Hills and Channel Islands in the distance.

"In order to give an idea of the immensity of the hotel, these facts and figures might be of interest. There are in the present hotel 444 rooms for guests in addition to 60 rooms for servants, and the total number is in the neighborhood of 600 which includes 76 in bungalows. Future additions to the hotel, which have been planned and will be built as rapidly as necessary, call for an additional 600 rooms, making the entire capacity of the completed plant about 1200 rooms. With this thought in mind, the dining room, kitchen, lobby and ballrooms have all been designed to take care of this.

"There are in this house 13 acres of actual floor space, two of which are covered by hand-made tile; 25,000 square feet of plate glass windows; 2,100 doors; 30 miles of plumbing pipes in the main building alone and 60 miles of telephone conduit; 400 bath tubs in bathrooms that are all tiled. Even the bathrooms have outside exposure. An unusual feature is that the closets in the rooms are not less than 5x6 feet in dimension, and in many rooms they range 7x10 feet!

"Flower boxes are one of the features of both interior and exterior of the building, such as are enjoyed in European countries, and more than a mile of these concrete containers were constructed right on the grounds.

"The main hotel connects with the villas by 1300 feet of pergolas all covered with palm leaves, and all planted to vines, shrubs and flowers which are produced in the nursery and the lath house. Three acres were put under cultivation for the purpose of propagating shrubs and flowers. Eight acres have been put in lawn. In order to give the place the appearance of having been in existence for a long time, a number of very old plantings have been made. These include two fifty year old Washington palms, located on the Seventh Street side of the house, brought all the way from Santa Monica, a distance of twenty miles, at a cost of more than $1,000. Forty full grown trees of various kinds, ranging anywhere from 40 to 50 feet were brought from different parts of the country and Hawaii. The most interesting, perhaps, was 8 orange trees in full bearing, about 12 years of age, and brought from the Pasadena estate of railroad magnate H.E. Huntington. Mr. McNeal Swasey was general superintendent of actual construction, with perhaps a hundred contractors and sub-contractors used on the job."

Early East Garden view

Rincon Villa, which housed John Barrymore, Scott and Zelda Fitzgerald, Rudolph Valentino and Carmel Myers...all at the same time. Plus some interesting visitors.

Rare Washington palms, part of extensive and exotic gardens.

New hotel with vintage cars.

Vernon Goodwin came to the Ambassador from the Alexandria. He proclaimed, "This hotel stands for the ultimate in hotel service and accomodation, and will be the center of the social life and color in Southern California. As many resorts in Europe are made famous by their hotels, so shall Los Angeles with its unsurpassable climate and great charm. The opening of the Ambassador will be a powerful magnet to attract the pleasure seeker, the investor, the house builder and the film maker. Its opening is an important milestone in ultimate development of this favored community."

Architect Myron Hunt agreed. "The Southwestern Coast is the playground of the country and draws thousands of tourists and winterers to its summer climate, but until the Ambassador, the immediate environs of Los Angeles contained no adequate answer of accomodation within the city whose consistent publicizing has turned a desert into a garden."

Grover Sholem supervised the interior decorating schemes and said that, "Sunlight is essential to the hotel as it is the embodiment of the spirit of California. People arriving here from the East wish to throw off their formalities and restraints and assume the carefree mantle of a more 'dolce far niente' way of living. So we brought the sunlight indoors."

Suites, some with private parlors and breakfast rooms were furnished in light woods and wicker, satins and cretonnes. Original paintings by well known California artists were used in all private and public rooms. Murals of famous California historical events adorned some of the banquettes.

The public rooms were laid out on majestic scales, for instance, the dining room covered over half an acre of floor space. Three sides were solidly walled with glass, with much greenery used.

The grand lobby was the greatest North America had even seen, boasting an enormous stone Italian fireplace, tapestries and cut velvet drapes, magnificent wrought iron, glittering crystal fish bowls and light colored upholstered and wicker furniture complimenting oriental carpets and magnificent crystal chandeliers.

The panelled ballroom was more formal with long and rich folds of crimson velour swathing the wide stage and partition boxes and windows.

The Tea Room, Parrot Porch and Zinnia Grill were specially designed for teas, cards, letter-writing and leisure, and were inhabited by parrots, canaries and multitudes of various flora and fauna.

The motion picture theatre, which was traditionally attended by members of the film colony, was of Pompeian elegance, with a curtain entirely hand embroidered, and a master organ built by the great artist, Robert Morton. First National Productions presented first run pictures and premieres. Said Grover Sholem, "One runs away with one's self in writing or talking about the Ambassador. There is so much to enjoy, so much to describe. My thoughts seem to be only the beginning of the story that might be written...some day. Perhaps some day someone may be inspired to write it." And 60 years later, someone finally has!

Mr. Sholem was concerned about the "wild and wooly stories which have circulated about astronomical rates, which are absolutely untrue. The very fact that the rates are so reasonable has brought a large number of prominent residents of Los Angeles to this house to establish permanent living quarters, and in a number of instances have had the rooms fitted up with their own furnishings. The American plan rate ranges from $10.00 per day up. It would be difficult for the average man or woman who has any kind of a home with servants to live at a correspondingly low rate.

"Not a new idea is a community of shops in connection with a great hotel, but it has been carried much farther here, with 37 exclusive shopkeepers occupying their own stores, many having both corridor and exterior entrances. Included is a Post Office, antique shop, furrier, broker's office, fine art gallery and I. Magnin for the latest in Milady's fashions."

Music, symphony, concert and dance was an important feature with daily concerts and dinner music, then dancing and social activities later. As guests wintered at the Ambassador, entertainment and excitement had to be sustained. In addition to scheduled activities, provided were a bowling alley, billiard room, sun porches for reading and writing, card rooms, outdoor pool and bath house, and a miniature golf course. A private school, play ground, inside nursery with attendants were provided for the young set.

To come later was the private club, where members could keep their private stock of bootleg booze, and where sophisticated guests were privvy to gambling activities.

The hotel's young chef, Rudolph Frie, formerly cooked for many of the crowned heads of Europe and was presented a medal by Empress Eugenie. Formerly of Paris, London and New York, as were his assistant chefs and catering department, they offered the finest cuisine and service to be had in California.

Top left clockwise: The Fiesta Dining Room (now Embassy Ballroom) with windows on three sides, "letting in the California sunshine, where one can see all the way to the Pacific Ocean"; private party room, one of several which boasted artistic hand drawn scenes of California; usherette costumes designed by Peggy Hamilton for the Ambassador Theatre: promenade of shops.

**Miniature golf course on the hotel grounds, where from hotel windows guests watched Howard Hughes, Katherine Hepburn and other stars at play.**

Writer Joe Minster exclaimed, "Vast, velvety lawns, flowers in profusion and trees bearing fruit make the Ambassador an oasis in the 'desert' of Wilshire Boulevard, all lending such charm to the establishment. Howard and Smith were the landscape artists who achieved this miracle."

"Over a million plants were propagated, and it was our custom to have fresh flowers daily in all of the rooms in addition to meeting guests at the train station with bouquets of flowers," remembered Frisco Mari 50 years later. Mari was a young immigrant Italian boy when he first worked during the opening of the hotel, later to become the chief gardener. Mari's affection and allegiance to the hotel continues through his lifetime...his story is remarkable...his subsequent wealth was derived from raising and selling Arabian horses for as high as $100,000 each...his first one a gift from the Cotton family who then owned the hotel, and the second from an Arabian king.

Personnel created a veritable city of itself. The vast accounting department, reservations, front desk, bellmen, engineers, carpenters, upholsterers, electricians, waiters, waitresses, laundry and garage attendants, gardeners and housekeeping department were all responsible for eminently high criteria of service, thus assuring the comfort of the guests. Hotel employees numbered over 1,000, and many guests travelled with their own staff who also enjoyed the hotel amenities.

Former Examiner reporter John B. Browne headed the publicity department. "In this establishment it is... of very vital interest and necessity. Our hotel administrators are acutely aware of the need for publicity and recognition," he allowed.

Stories, escapades and excitement literally poured out of the "new hotel which has become the brightest light on the West Coast...and Mr. Browne makes hay with it. Browne's staff is almost as large as that of the average city editor on a newspaper!", so commented the publication of the Los Angeles Press Club...which was soon to make its home in the hotel.

*Anything* that took place at the hotel was front page news. One of the amusing incidents to make coast-to-coast headlines was when a guest uncovered a real pearl in her oyster at a dinner party.

Revues claimed, "Hosting Presidents, royalty, the rich and famous, travelers from every country and glamourous performers and luminaries of the cinema, the hotel quickly crowned a new social era and set a precedent in the brilliance for Southern California".

Now that was news.

A PAGE OF FAIR AMBASSADOR WOMEN

*Mrs. Charles Jeffras, the hostess, a well-known society woman of Southern California.*

*Mrs. Adelaide S. Plunkett, one of the keenest housekeepers in America*

*Three charming aides in Ambassador service—Miss Ora Johnson, an able publicity lady; Miss Al Dean Shockley, diplomatic secretary of Manager Banks, and Miss Goldie Palmer, chief of the telephone department.*

**"Fair Ambassador women in our service" (in earlier years).**

*"Congratulations!"*

*The two young genuises on whom rested the greatest responsibilities of the $5,000,000 Ambassador enterprise, on New Year's morning were able to shake hands. They opened the house on schedule. Grover A. Sholem and William F. Banks in their working clothes, wearing also smiles of relief over accomplished results.*

# A Happy New Year

It was the last day of the year, and as building debris was still being carried away...the clock struck midnight. Bells and horns sounded to welcome in the New Year, and the Ambassador threw open its doors and made its official and promised appearance. The date was January 1, 1921.

Up until the last stroke of the clock, maids, porters, bellmen, waiters and all had been rushing around shoving furniture and fixtures into place because of a last minute crisis. Two days before there had not been a sign of carpets, furniture, lights, fixtures, drapes in the lobby, dining room or ballrooms...much less linens, mattresses or furniture in the guest rooms. Nothing had arrived on time.

Outside, masses of wreckage and great piles of earth were being cleared away from the main entrance by a tractor which was followed by a steam roller giving the decomposed granite a hard, even surface.

Working 36 consecutive hours...the steam roller's last sweep which allowed for the hotel's first paths and driveways, was followed by a "blooming" Englishman fresh off the boat from London, who strolled into the hotel not caring whether accomodations were ready or not, but determined to register.

With all due courtesy and great flourishes of pomp and ceremony, the gentleman was shown to his room. He was not to be alone. The hotel was prepared to accommodate 300 additional guests... *ten minutes* before the proposed opening time.

Amidst the shouts of "Happy New Year" and sounds of firecrackers and bells, the great lady made her debut as the collapsing crew rejoiced. They deserved to celebrate...and did...all except Goldie Palmer and her telephone operators. Switchboard power had gone out and they were ringing phones via an old-fashioned hand crank.

This was the first resort hotel established in the entire region, complete with bridle paths, riding rink and stables, miles of garden paths, an Olympic-sized outdoor swimming pool, a miniature golf course snaking round the grassy grounds, and the hotel's own Rancho Country Club and golf course nearby with continuous limousine transportation. Guests were privileged to use the nearby landing field at Wilshire and Fairfax for the new-mode transportation... *airplanes.* And the soon to be added tennis courts combined to make the Ambassador the peer of luxury resort hotels in the entire nation.

And it all took root on land considered undesirable because it rose to a little hill.

"Somebody said that it couldn't be done,
But he, with a chuckle, replied
That 'maybe it couldn't,' but he would be one
Who wouldn't say so till he'd tried.
So he buckled right in, with the trace of a grin
On his face. If he worried, he hid it.
He started to sing as he tackled the thing
That couldn't be done, and he did it.

"Somebody scoffed: 'Oh, you'll never do that;
At least, no one ever has done it.'
But he took off his coat and took off his hat,
And the first thing we knew he'd begun it;
With the lift of his chin, and a bit of a grin,
Without any doubting or quiddit,
He started to sing as he tackled the thing
That couldn't be done, and he did it.

"There are thousands to tell you it cannot be done.
There are thousands to prophesy failure;
There are thousands to point out to you, one by one,
The dangers that wait to assail you;
But just tackle it with a bit of a grin,
Then take off your coat and go to it;
Just start in to sing as you tackle the thing
That 'cannot be done,' and you'll do it."

Poem posted by grateful management for hard-working employees success.

Los Angeles Sunday Times

...MORNING, JANUARY 16, 1921. | THE ONLY NEWSPAPER ROTOGRAVURE SECTION WEST OF THE ROCKIES | LAST WORD IN MODERN PRINT...

*The New Ambassador Hotel (Formerly the California) in the Wilshire District.*

THIS MAGNIFICENT PILE OCCUPIES A SITE THAT WAS A BARLEY FIELD A FEW YEARS AGO

*Formal Launching of Magnificent Hotel Crowns New Social Era Here*

The Examiner reported, "The splendor of the setting for the affair probably has never been equalled on the Pacific Coast. Never has a society event in the South seen so many dinner parties gathered under one roof, and probably never before have so many orchestras been assembled together in one room, each carrying the same melody in complete harmony."

While uniformed attendants of the hotel were sweeping the ankle-deep confetti from the ballrooms the "morning after" the exciting event of January 18, 1921, Angelenos were reading about who attended and of the gowns the distinguished ladies wore in their Los Angeles Times, the Examiner and other dailies statewide.

Great, lengthy, flowery descriptions enthused over the garlands of flowers "in the dead of winter". The cuisine was "admirable" European in nature and each course a surprise and at each place a corsage or boutonniere.

The men were appropriately attired in formal tails and tuxedos, and the affair was remarkable for the gorgeous costumes of the ladies. Guests included several prominent visitors to the city from far-off and foreign ports as well as most of the local society leaders. Mrs. William McAdoo, wife of the Secretary of the Treasury, Mrs. Edward Laurence Doheny, Mrs. Hancock Banning, Mrs. William Preston Harrison, Mrs. Leo Phillips, Mrs. Wayland Morrison, Miss Florence Marsh, Mrs. Marshall Wellborn, Mrs. William Garland, Mrs. W. W. Mines, Mrs. I. N. Van Nuys, Mrs. Richard Jewett Schweppe, Mrs. William Furst and Miss Mary Dockweiler were some of the ladies whose gowns of velvet, taffeta, satin, chiffon, brocade and tulle were complimented by ostrich feathered fans, and pearl, emerald and diamond studded jeweled bracelets, necklaces and tiaras, and their furs of sable, mink and ermine.

But you'll note. No theatrical names or film stars included on the social scene...yet.

Westways Magazine later reported "The Ambassador burst on the scene when Wilshire Boulevard was still a narrow unpaved street. It preempted the luxury hotel field and became, almost immediately, the gathering place of Southern California Society.

"Los Angeles' modern era was opened by the Ambassador Hotel and the Cocoanut Grove".

From the time of that fabulous opening, the Hotel has hosted some of the city's brightest social events and grandest celebrations.

It has been the scene of Academy Award presentations, Golden Globe Awardings, location for many motion picture and television filmings and gala Hollywood events where stars, Wall Street financiers, high society and royalty rubbed elbows.

★ ★ ★

## BRILLIANT SCENE MARKS AMBASSADOR'S OPENING.

*Three Thousand Persons, Including Vast Array of Gorgeously Gowned Women, Make Event Notable.*

# A Metropolis...and The Ladies Emerge

"Los Angeles did not really get her post-war stride until the year 1921. Then, indeed, the old Pueblo stepped out on the 'Big Time' circuit and took her place among America's metropolitan cities. As a portent of a whole series of unique events to come, the Ambassador Hotel, one of the largest tourist and convention hotels in the country, opened," reported historian Laurance Hill in LA REINA.

"Not to be outdone by Mother Nature, the event was followed a few days later by a snowstorm in Hollywood and a display of the Aurora Borealis over the Sierra Madres. The snow, which stood a whole day before melting, spoiled some perfectly good subtropical South Sea Island movie sets, and the northern lights, first and last ever seen here, seriously interfered with our modern telephone and telegraph transmission."

USC and UCLA played their first game in the newly built Los Angeles Coliseum in November of 1923 filling its 80,000 seats for the first time compared to the previous audiences of 12,000 in other facilities. The Coliseum's advent opened the way to the acceptance of William M. Garland's invitation to the Olympic Committee in Antwerp, to host the 1932 Olympiad in this fair city.

Culture and leisure were staying abreast of the activity in the city as Henry Huntington bought Gainsborough's famous painting, "The Blue Boy" which still can be seen in the Huntington Library. Newcomers flocked to the sparkling beaches from their inland and arid states...and religion? Billy Sunday rivaled the beaches as an attraction with his stirring hell-fire and brimstone sermons on the city's day of rest.

Digging for new homes and oil-well structures set off a flurry of activity reaching such intensity that bankers and businessmen felt that the peak of the city's growth had been reached...in 1923.

Meanwhile, Los Angeles Women...whose charitable motivations have never diminished, were volunteering aid by way of fund-raisers for Japanese earthquake sufferers and starving German children to the tune of millions of dollars.

The ladies' society endeavors increased appreciably, bringing culture, music, art, and a western "400" into prominence...as well as inching the door open further in the worlds of industry and business into which they had been thrust by their war work efforts.

William Jennings Bryan was spending the summer at the Ambassador where he witnessed the famous debate of Adela Rogers St. Johns and Alice Ames Winter, the President of the General Federation of Women's Clubs, as it took place under the watchful eye of Adela's publisher and boss, William Randolph Hearst and his paramour Marion Davies.

**Adela Rogers St. Johns, career woman; at her typewriter with Tyrone Power; and interviewing the Duke and Duchess of Windsor, after David had abdicated the throne of England for "the woman I love".**

"Is Modern Woman A Failure?" Adela asked, referring to women of that period entering the business world. Taking the position that "indeed they are," Adela won the debate...even though she herself was successfuly "driving the three mules of home, motherhood and *career.*"

"Newspaperman" as she called herself, Adela, meanwhile was writing magazine short stories which were also being sold as motion picture scripts. An intimate of all of the early stars, she became known as their "Mother Confessor", and as such, was the first editor of PHOTOPLAY MAGAZINE, dedicated to chronicling the lives, affairs and peccadillos of the stars. Motion pictures were rapidly becoming the number one industry in California.

# Fashions Viewed at The Ambassador

Fashion arbiter Peggy Hamilton with internationally famous dancing star Irene Castle. They're carrying dolls that were the fashion craze.

Miss Hamilton began the Los Angeles Times rotogravure section and was the earliest person to visualize the city as a fashion center.

Miss Hamilton in sports clothes.

Lily Damita wearing a stylish cloche hat.

Film star Irene Rich in a tea gown.

# Good Neighbor Hollywood

*HOLLYWOOD*

*Hollywood, Hollywood...*
*Fabulous Hollywood...*
*Celluloid Babylon,*
*Glorious, glamorous...*
*City delirious,*
*Frivolous, serious...*
*Bold and ambitious,*
*Vicious, delicious.*
*Drama—a city-full,*
*Tragic and pitiful...*
*Bunk, junk, and genius*
*Amazingly blended...*
*Tawdry, tremendous,*
*Absurd, stupendous;*
*And astonishiingly splendid...*
*HOLLYWOOD!*
*DON BLANDING*

*(As recited by Leo Carillo in the 1935 Colortone Musical, "Star Night at the Cocoanut Grove.")*

★ ★ ★

Stories emanating from any hotel in the world are bound, by the very nature of this personal and human business and its attendant services, to be bursting with drama, intrigue, thrills, sex, glamour, pathos and disappointment. Moreso at the Ambassador.

Because, add to the scenario, her next door neighbor, Hollywood.

Early on, the two were bedfellows, and although it is not to say one wouldn't have survived without the other, certainly it must be allowed that both the hotel and Hollywood courted, supported, and needed each other for their growth and development. This in the days when actors existed in boarding houses and transient facilities...before luxurious, or even adequate producers and movie stars elegant diggings were built. The Ambassador was the place to entertain and to be entertained. A home away from home.

If Hollywood was the dream and work shop of the motion picture explosion, the Ambassador Hotel was the bedroom and living room of the industry. Stars, writers, directors and producers traditionally first saw the light of Hollywood day if they were sufficiently VIP to be chauffeured by the studio to the hotel or to finally "arrive" there after experiencing some successes in the movie world.

Like a proud, supportive parent, the Ambassador provided the nourishment, encouragement, rest and recreation, tea and sympathy, the luxury of palms and gardens and swimming pools and tennis courts required by the movie colony that had migrated to California...the land of blue skies and sunshine that had wooed and won them...as Hollywood developed and exploded into the most intriguing, influential-real, mythical-reel city in the world.

THE AMBASSADOR HOTEL'S WORLD FAMOUS

# COCOANUT GROVE

## "Putting On My Top Hat, Tying Up My White Tie, Dancing In My Tails"

The Ambassador lobby was teaming with a rich, colorful, top-hatted white tie, tails and tuxedoed group of men with elegantly gowned, feathered and bejeweled ladies on their arms.

Excitement was at a crescendo. The hotel management had caught the imagination of the public by stealthily planning a new room "for dining and dancing pleasure" without divulging motif, decor or policy and they had all been invited to the grand opening.

It's predecessor, Los Angeles' first night club, the "Zinnia Grill" had opened in the Ambassador months before. The club was located on the Casino level of the hotel, and its decor of black polished satin on which was painted a profusion of Zinnias soon was affectionately nicknamed "The Black Patent Leather Room" by its devotees. There was a need for the early film personalities and hard-working city fathers to play. This was the answer, and the room was an immediate success.

At that time, the city was just entering its period of rapid growth. The film industry was commencing to grow equally fast, producing the "Hollywood" of fame and fortune. A mere few miles further west of the Ambassador on Wilshire Boulevard, where the Prudential Plaza is now, one could board the Goodyear blimp for a balloon ride over the city, and just west of the La Brea Tar Pits, with its bubbling oil, mud, tar and mastodons at Wilshire and Fairfax, now the site of the May Company and Ohrbach's, planes were taking off and landing on Sidney Chaplin's air field. Even more remote, traveling west to the sea, was La Cienega (which in Spanish translates to "the swamp") a boulevard now noted as Restaurant Row. Further west Beverly Hills was still primarily agricultural.

But society was coming alive at the Ambassador, and the enthusiastic audiences in the small Zinnia Grill, with its long lines of patrons queing up waiting to get in to dine and dance, precipitated management to convert the Grand Ballroom into a first-class nightclub.

And so it was that on the night of April 21, 1921 when the new club officially opened its Moroccan style, gold leaf and etched palm tree doors, it was to a standing-room only audience.

The "COCOANUT GROVE" was aptly named, guests agreed as they were escorted by the maitre'd and captains down the wide plush grand staircase (perfect for "making entrances" stars and celebrities soon learned) to their reserved tables. Overhead, soaring about the room were cocoanut trees of papier maché, cocoanuts and palm fronds which had been rescued from the sandy beaches of Oxnard where they had served as atmosphere for Rudolph Valentino's film of the 1921 classic, "The Sheik." Swinging from their branches were stuffed monkeys blinking at the revelers with their electrified amber eyes. Stars twinkled in the blue ceiling sky, and on the southernmost wall hung a full Hawaiian moon presiding over a painted landscape and splashing waterfall.

★ ★ ★

The Cocoanut Grove, its soon-to-become famous waterfall and exotic palm trees suggested and provided by Rudolph Valentino from his film "The Sheik." Rudy, "an American heart throb," was a long time resident of the Ambassador.

Mae West...making an "entrance".

It was no illusion. Into the city of make-believe, a tropical island had moved, and from its very beginning, the "fabulous" Cocoanut Grove was destined to become tradition, trademark, landmark and trysting place to Los Angeles. A way of life which was to continue for over half a century. Music styles and trends through the years can be documented via the Room's entertainment bookings.

Opening with the most popular jazz band of the day, Art Hickman, who, according to Great Dance Band historian Leo Walker, was the first to attract national attention, the Grove established a precedent that was never to waver...that of securing the very best in entertainment for the room. Hickman's engagement lasted for months, as did the bands of Abe Lyman and Gus Arnheim who followed him, simply because it was the beginning of the big band era and there were not too many of them in existence.

Coinciding with the Grove excitement, was the first roar of the Twenties with a cast of fun-loving sheiks and flappers with their extended cigarette holders, silver flasks, "knee peeking" skirts and razzmatazz floppy pants. Resident author Scott Fitzgerald called it, "the greatest, gaudiest spree in American history".

Gus Arnheim and his orchestra.

Jimmy Grier and his orchestra. The trio, "Three Ambassadors" included "smiling" Jack Smith. They replaced Bing Crosby and the Rhythm Boys. Arnheim discovered them at Hollywood High School.

Extraordinary Announcement!

The AMBASSADOR takes pleasure in announcing that the Incomparable Danseuse –

# Mrs. Irene Castle!

ASSISTED BY

## Mr. William Reardon

will open a two week engagement at The "COCOANUT GROVE" commencing with a DINNER DANCE DE-LUXE on Monday Evening February 19th

Reservations may now be made for Opening Night Dinner Six Dollars per person including Couvert. For the remainder of this engagement couvert charges will be 1.00 per person except on Tuesdays and Saturdays 1.50

New Numbers
to be presented by
MRS. CASTLE
will include
her alluring
"Midsummer Night's Dream Waltz"
"Flirtation Walk"
New "Castle One Step"
& "Swing Along"

Mrs. Castle's Gowns
Designed by
Frances and Co.,
New York
&
Molyneaux, Paris

Lyman's
All-Star Orchestra

On Wednesday Afternoons, Feb. 21st and 28th
A Special
IRENE CASTLE—*The Dansant*
will be given in the
Orange Tea Room *of* The Ambassador
at which Mrs. Castle will appear
in dances with Mr. Reardon.

"Star Night" and W.C. Fields, Fanny Brice and Eddie Cantor warming up their act. Anita Page with Jimmy Durante. Orchestra leader Phil Harris.

Jean Harlow with Guy Lombardo. Marie Dressler with Jean Harlow. Phil Harris with Claudette Colbert; Genevieve Tobin and Cecil B. DeMille.

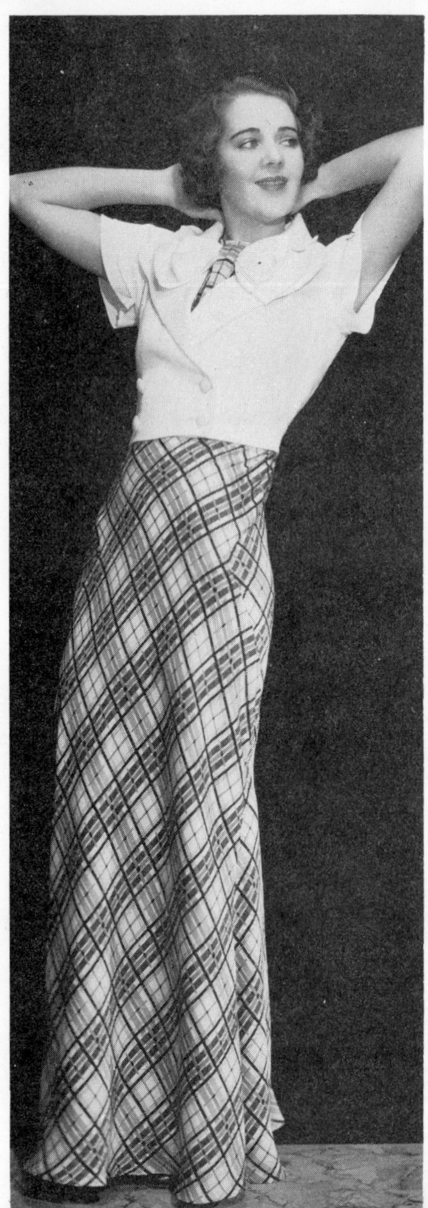

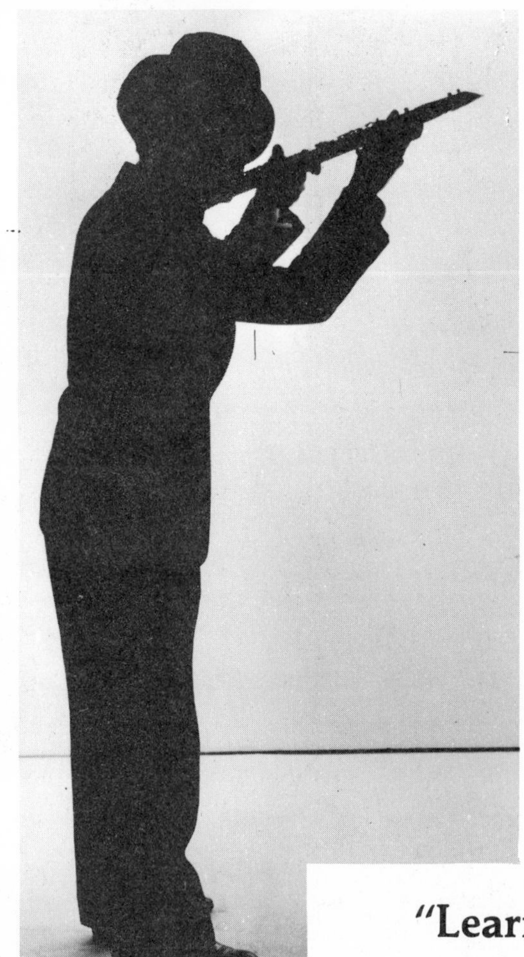

Ruby Keeler, musical star. (wife of Al Jolson)

Orchestra leader Ted Lewis asking his familiar "Is everybody happy?"

Film star Carole Lombard with Crooner Russ Columbo to whom she was engaged. An accidental bullet from the gun of his best friend Lansing Brown, killed Columbo. Carole corresponded with Russ' mother until the frail lady's death, so that she would not learn that he was dead.

## "Learn to Croon"

Gus Arnheim "coming to you from the world-famous Cocoanut Grove...entertainer to the stars, and star of the entertainers" featured the Rhythm Boys, one of whom was indisputably the first live entertainer to become idolized as were exciting Sinatra, Presley and the Beatles to follow. The Rhythm Boys were Harry Barris, Al Rinker and the one and only *Bing Crosby*. Also soloing with Arnheim were Donald Novis, Loyce Whiteman and a young violinist named Russ Columbo...a keen competitor to Crosby's crooning fame.

The Grove, in retrospect, was considered responsible for bringing together for the first time, the worlds of society and show business. Together, fun-loving guests enjoyed the music of Ted Lewis and Paul Whiteman, Jimmie Grier, Mal Hallett and Jackie Taylor...

January 26, 1922 marked the scheduling of the first floor show. A packed house welcomed Maurice and Leonora Hughes...the rage of Paris, London and New York, where they had performed their famous skating waltz before such crowned heads as King George of England, King Alphonso of Spain and King Albert of Belgium. Los Angeles was "on the map".

Since world renowned entertainers were not as numerous nor available in those days, it was several months after this engagement ended, that the Grove was able to obtain one of wonders of the day—Sidar Ramma Setti, the greatest exponent of mental telepathy of that

The Rhythm Boys... Harry Barris, Bing Crosby and Al Rinker appearing at the Cocoanut Grove. Bing soloed... was heard coast-to-coast... and became famous!

era. After he had delved into the innermost thoughts of all of our socialites and left these shores, along came (in October of 1922) the "Great Night Frolic". The "Frolic" was produced by Joseph K. Gorham, (affectionately known as Florenz Ziegfeld, Jr). Coupled with Abe Lyman's irresistible music and his All-Star orchestra, twenty beauties packed the Grove night after night, for a long engagement.

Not long after came those hectic days and the world-resounding roar of Hollywood's glamour years, that golden era when the motion picture industry came into its own and audience participation became the order of the day.

"States Nights" were inaugurated on Tuesday evenings. On Friday evenings the Grove reverberated with the fight songs of U.S.C., California and U.C.L.A., when patrons came to celebrate "College Night" and exult in victory or drown their sorrows in defeat.

Such stars as the "Duncan Sisters", Dawn Roland, the twinkling dancing feet of the "Abbott Dancers", Mabel Normand, Barbara La Marr, Dolores del Rio and Lupe Velez were nightly participants at these parties where Hollywood played.

## "Don't Bring Lulu"

Other starlets of the day who became famous were Grove regulars: Gloria Swanson, Mary Pickford, the Bennett Sisters, the Talmadge Sisters, Barbara Stanwyck and Joan Crawford. All often coming stag.

"Stars Night" ... World champion boxer Jack Dempsey in an act with orchestra leader Jackie Taylor.

"Beautiful little wildcat" Joan Crawford.

*ANOTHER STAR IN THE ASCENDANT.*
*Miss Gretchen Young, most youthful of a triad of charming sisters, who are faithful patrons of the "Cocoanut Grove," particularly on College Nights, has just signed an enviable contract with First National.*

## "Charleston-Charleston"

Grove dancing contests became popular among the young movie set. It was the place to see and be seen.

No one who ever saw her dance could forget the starlet who danced away with most of the trophies...Lucille Le Sueur, that "beautiful little wildcat", later to become famous as Joan Crawford.

One of Joan's favorite dancing partners was socialite Mike Cudahy...melding his ceremonious world with hers of show business. But for the interference of his proper and Victorian mother, they would have married, wrote Adela Rogers St. Johns.

Popular deb Lucy Toberman remembers that the judges included Charles Chaplin, Jesse Lasky and L.B. Mayer among others, and they were as exciting as the contestants. With her hotly won trophies under her arm, Lucy would always be reminded by the waiters when it was the bewitching hour of midnight...and to go home as she attended regular classes at UCLA.

Others vying in the contests were Gloria Swanson, Mary Pickford, Joan Bennett, Constance Bennett, Barbara Stanwyck, Carole Lombard, Dorothy Manners, Dorothy Lamour, Loretta Young, little sister of Sally Blane and Polly Ann Young.

## "Baby Face"

Dorothy Manners, a long-time Los Angeles Herald Examiner movie columnist, was one of a group of young girls who attended the Grove regularly. "Joan Crawford was our 'ringleader'. On Saturdays, we girls would gather together for the Grove's weekly Tea Dances," she remembered.

"As usual, we stopped by for Sally Blane and Polly Ann Young, and their mother told them that they couldn't go if they didn't take their little 15-year old sister. We obliged, and danced off. 'Little sister' wore a filmy, soft and flowing gown and wide brimmed picture hat framing quite the lovliest face the Grove regulars had ever seen. Coming down the grand staircase, she was the very essence of beauty.

"Although Joan had her usual table No. 1...it was deadly...we didn't get much attention of our own that day. The vision of beauty was Loretta Young.

"Joan was furious. She said, 'Never again'! I don't know if she ever forgave Loretta for being so beautiful."

Wampus Baby Stars at the pool: L-R, Mrs. Reginald Denny, Helen Ferguson, Sybil Brand, Ruth Roland, Laura LaPlante, and Ruth Clifford.

"Wampas Baby Stars" elected annually by the Western Associated Motion Picture Advertisers, had its beginning in 1922 with Colleen Moore topping the list.

## "Ain't We Got Fun"

The Cocoanut Grove accounted for the West's first mingling of old-guard society and the Hollywood community...encouraged by Mrs. Clyde Russell Burr (Alice Hicks) as she formed the "Twenty Little Working Girls" to headline in the nightclub for a long period. Their most festive performances were fashion shows and the annual Champagne Ball. One theme was "The Vintage Years" indicative of pre-Depression times. A pageant of wines was held. The "Little Working Girls" were costumed as popular songs, historical events, and the fashions of previous years...thus combining society, history, and show-biz.

The "Wampus Baby Stars" was entertainment provided by a galaxy of established stars, featuring Maurice Chevalier, Will Rogers, Tom Mix, Jeanette MacDonald, Jimmy Durante, and the Duncan Sisters. The festivities were M.C.'d by actor Frank Fay and the stage manager was Chinese Theatre owner Sid Grauman.

## "Baby, It's Cold Outside"

Often, members of the audience were as important as the entertainment, sometimes more so. First-nighters included: Ben Lyon, Lionel Barrymore, Harold Lloyd, Frederick March, John Barrymore, matinee idols Maurice Costello, Antonio Moreno, Rudolph Valentino, John Gilbert and Douglas Fairbanks...and the very private Greta Garbo.

The keynote was extravagance. Any stunt was feasible, no matter how absurd it was. "Hobby Horse Races" featured attractive young starlets riding hobby horses across the dance floor in races as hotly contested as any at Santa Anita...with admirers betting heavily on their favorites.

New Year's Eve in the Grove was possibly more hectic and hilarious than at any other time. One favorite midnight stunt was to freeze scantily clad bathing beauties in glasses of ice and lower them from the ceiling at the stroke of twelve. One year, the stunt backfired when one cake of ice froze somewhat too solidly, and the girl inside was turning blue by the time they finally chipped her out.

More than anything else, the Grove is remembered by capricious, whimsical, extravagant features and stunts, as well as its sterling entertainment which has highlighted more than 15,000 nights of fun and frolic in the room.

Peggy Hamilton, the official hostess for the 1932 Olympics in Los Angeles with Governor James Rolph.

# "Animal Crackers"

John Barrymore and his drinking buddy W.C. Fields nightly could be found at their same table entertaining the audience with their own brands of comedy and craziness. Barrymore's pet monkey mingled with the monkey dolls that hung from the palms about the room. But brother Lionel went him one better by bringing in seven one evening and setting them loose in the room. Customers went wild, started jumping to reach the monkeys...and the Monkey Dance was born to flourish briefly, and again come into fashion in the 70's!

Early in the Grove's history, one evening a sketch of Barney Google and Sparkplug by their mentor Billie De Beck was autographed by the glamorous assemblage and auctioned off for $5,000.

"The Musical Enchantress" Lily Pons meeting Minnie and Mickey Mouse on their tenth birthday.

Trumpets blared and flags flew on August 3rd, 1932, when the Grove became the scene of the spectacular "Ball of All Nations", honoring prominent visitors from all over the world to the Xth Olympiad. The honorary committee included the then Governor of California, James Rolph Jr., Mr. and Mrs. William May Garland, Mrs. Hancock Banning — social arbiter of the period. Under the direction of Ernest Belcher (father of Marge Champion), a special Grecian and American Ballet was featured.

It was on October 4, 1930, that a gala party was held in the Grove celebrating the second birthday of beloved Mickey Mouse, Minnie Mouse, Pluto, Clarabelle, et al, together with their father Walt Disney — to receive the felicitations of civic, society leaders and the elite of filmdom.

Marian Davies (who lived with William Randolph Hearst in the entire east wing of the second floor for a year) rode a white horse through the lobby to a costume party in the Cocoanut Grove for the amusement of her lover. When asked if he was surprised, his answer was, "Yes, indeed. She hates horses!"

Popular and enduring ballroom dance duo, Veloz and Yolanda.

Resident William Randolph Hearst with Irene Dunne, Bette Davis, Louella Parsons presiding over one of the publisher's many costume parties.

Phil Harris and his orchestra. It became a tradition for featured bands to be photographed on the expansive hotel lawn.

1939 saw a rearrangement of the room. Tiers at the south end were covered and the boxes (which Grove regulars had reserved on an annual basis as in theatres) were closed...to be used no more. It reopened with a huge charity party sponsored by the Assistance League of Los Angeles. The floor show starred famous Veloz and Yolanda, Coleman Clark and his famous ping pong players, with Anson Weeks Orchestra.

Among the many orchestras appearing in the Grove in this decade were Bob Denton, Johnny Hampton, Ted Fio Rito, Jimmy Grier, Phil Harris, Guy Lombardo, Sid Lipmann, Henry Busse, Eddie Duchin, Ozzie Nelson, Hal Grayson, Shep Fields, Rudy Vallee, Paul Whiteman, Hal Kemp and others...and of course Freddy Martin.

★ ★ ★

# "The Tschaikowsky And Martin Serenade"

FREDDY MARTIN'S REFLECTIONS

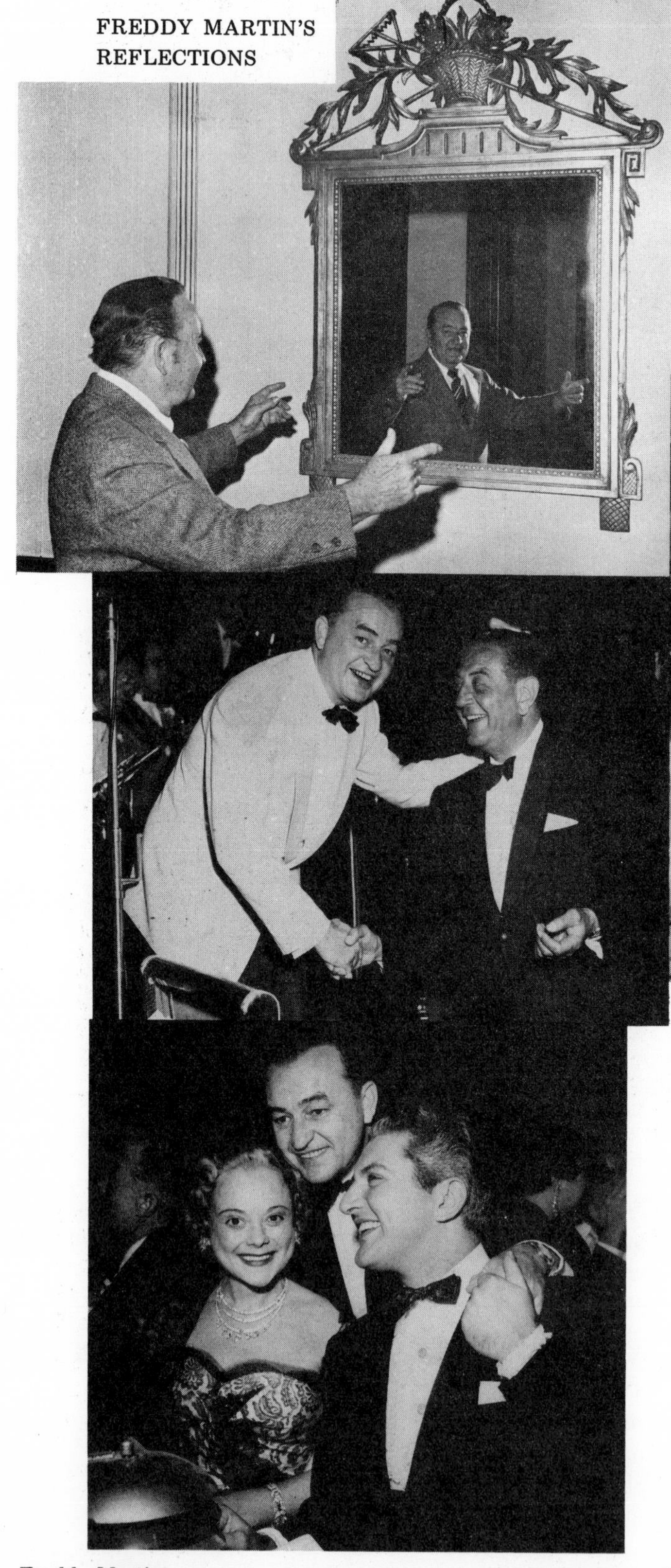

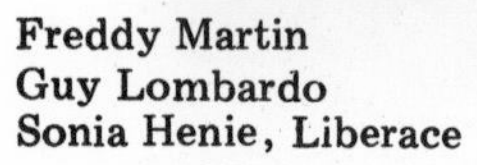

Freddy Martin
Guy Lombardo
Sonia Henie, Liberace

George Montgomery, Buddy Clark, Dinah Shore
Xaviar Cugat
Rudy Vallee

Freddy Martin, "Mr. Cocoanut Grove to thousands of dancing and romancing couples played the room for weeks and months of every year from 1938 to 1970. In 1941 he unearthed a musical mother lode that within a matter of weeks made him one of the most popular orchestra leaders in the nation. The bonanza was Tschaikowsky's "Piano Concerto in B Flat Minor" which he arranged and recorded as a 32-bar dance version titled "Tonight We Love." It was an immediate hit, and sold over 3 million copies. He adopted it as his theme song, and followed it with other classics: "Symphony," the Grieg and Rachmaninoff piano concertos, "Warsaw Concerto" as dance favorites, and the "Sabre Dance" and "Flight of the Bumble Bee," into Boogie-woogie renditions.

Pat Boone
The Martin Men (MervGriffin in the center),
Bobby Breen

James Cagney
Elizabeth Taylor
Peter Duchin
Alice Faye, Phil Harris

# Merv and Freddy

Freddy Martin and Merv Griffin

**Giving up a lucrative radio career ($1500 per week) to accept a job as vocalist and second piano player ($175 per week) with Freddy Martin's Band a young Merv Griffin soon received national exposure and acclaim.**
**A favorite with Grove patrons, one of Merv's most avid fans was Howard Hughes. Now older, a billionaire, and considered eccentric, Hughes would take a table in the back of the Grove, order vanilla ice cream, and listen to Merv.**

"Remember when Judy Garland, who had been ill for several years and had been undergoing psychiatric and alcoholic treatment? She had not been doing any entertaining for quite some time when Gus Lampe, the Grove's entertainment director believed that Judy could reestablish herself, so he signed her. To my surprise she came to me and asked if I could conduct for her. I jumped at the chance and the little girl with the big voice enjoyed a smashing engagement.

"On her closing night we cut an album. Usually this would take three or four sessions, but we accomplished it in one take. It was titled, 'Judy at the Grove', and became a best seller.

"The dance team of Veloz and Yolanda used to conduct competitions at the Grove, and I vividly remember the night the contest was won by Gower Champion... who has since achieved fame as a dancer, dance director and now famous stage and screen director. Another Grove discovery.

"During the World War II years we used to invite any customer buying a war bond to conduct the orchestra in a number. It was fun when they would direct a simple number, but," Freddy laughed, "we were in big trouble when amateurs decided to direct 'Rhapsody in Blue' or Tschaikowsky.

"When Mickey Rooney was in the room, he was always welcome to sit in on drums.He was very good as the whole world could see during a spontaneous performance on an Academy Award night."

**"Judy at the Grove" before an SRO audience of her adoring fans, Judy made a comeback.**
**Judy's famous and favorite album recorded in one take accompanied by Freddy and his band on her closing night in the Grove. Now a collector's item, it was borrowed from a close young friend of Judy's...Holly Raines.**

# GALA PARTY-
## Franco-British War Relief

• COCOANUT GROVE—famous rendezvous in the Los Angeles Ambassador for the picture people of filmdom's capital—was the setting for the recent Franco-British War Relief Dinner Dance. Members of the British-French colonies in Hollywood and Beverly Hills joined as sponsors and the distinguished Stars who attended—"great was the host of them." Not only did they attend but they performed and entertained for the amusement of each other. It was one of the most brilliant and outstanding parties ever given. This remarkably fine photograph of the "Grove" was taken just as a group of famous actors were doing "The Man on the Flying Trapeze." You will recognize most of them but from left to right they are: Ian Hunter, Herbert Marshall, Nigel Bruce, Ralph Forbes, Alan Mowbray, William Powell, Lawrence Olivier, Reginald Gardiner, Ronald Colman, Charles Laughton, Adolph Menjou, Charles Boyer, and Richard Barthelmess.

Ray Noble and his orchestra were appearing at the Grove when World War II engulfed the nation in 1941. Immediately the venerable Grove, ever ready to lend a hand, rang with cries for War Bonds, help for the Red Cross and U.S.O.'s. Even before the United States entered the war, it was doing its part as the scene for numerous British and French War Relief groups.

*Ray Noble, with Ann Sothern, at Ambassador Hotel in Los Angeles in 1941.*

• FLOWER-GIRL'S proceeds go to the war relief fund. Ronald Colman points a warning finger at the photographer as he listens to Claudette Colbert's sales-talk for her posies.

—Weaver

• GLEEFUL CHATTERERS are Mrs. Charles Boyer (Pat Patterson) and Charles Laughton.

• HONEYMOONERS attending—William Powell and his lovely bride, Diana Lewis.

• ANOTHER FLOWER GIRL, Maureen O'Sullivan sells to Reginald Gardiner.

—Len Weissman Photographs

# "Don't Sit Under the Apple Tree With Anyone Else But Me"

Margaret's date Loren O'Dell was in uniform also.

**WAR YEARS. Actress Jane Withers celebrating her 17th birthday at the Cocoanut Grove with young friends: Dick Clayton, Sheila O'Malley, John Kimball, Thelma Mundy, Sgt. Bill Shirley, Judy Clark, Sgt. Jack Watson, Elaine Sonn, Joe Brown, Jr., Jeanne Hawlett, Gene Cole, Kathleen O'Malley and Farley Granger.**

At this time, the Grove was a mecca for service men who clamored to spend an evening inside its glamourous walls, giving them something to write home about, and a bright and warm memory to carry with them during their dreary days ahead. Movie stars always were on hand to dance with the servicemen, and to quell their loneliness.

Jan Savitt, Del Courtney, Eddie Oliver, Orrin Tucker, Carmen Cavallaro, Jack Fina, Emil Coleman, Eddie Fitzpatrick, Ray Hackett, Skitch Henderson, Horace Heidt and Harry James were some of the popular orchestras featured.

1943 saw the last of the several Academy Award Oscar presentations that had taken place at the Cocoanut Grove. Vast radio audiences, along with newspapers and magazines from all over the world were privy to thrill with the great gatherings of stars and celebrities.

Toward the end of the war, the public's appetite for "name entertainment" continued to grow. Returning servicemen had become accustomed to the best via the USO, and everyone was in a mood to celebrate.

So it was that such great names as Hildegarde, Dorothy Shay, Frankie Laine, Victor Borge, Peter Lind Hayes and Mary Healy began to appear on the famous Cocoanut Grove marquee. As entertainers and their stature grew and accelerated, so did entertainment at the Grove.

The fifties continued to bring big names: Dinah Shore, Tony Martin, Eddie Fisher, Harry Belafonte, Gloria de Haven, Constance Moore, Peggy Lee, Marge and Gower Champion, Jane Powell, Mickey Rooney, Vic Damone, Marguerite Piazza, Lena Horne, Frank Sinatra, the famous French singing star, Patacholl, Paul Neighbors and Gene Nelson. Nat King Cole and Judy Garland, among others. Judy long remembered the engagement as her "comeback" offered by the Grove when everyone else thought she was finished.

**Actor Brian Aherne greeting mother and daughter WAVE recruits Margaret and Evelyn Gilbert (of Pasadena).**

The Grove evokes fond memories for most, but one wonders what was going through the mind of Rita Hayworth when she was again at the Grove on the occasion of the Ambassador's Golden anniversary party...or of Haymes when in the 70's he again starred after many troublesome years, divorces and exiling himself to Europe. On each occasion, even though years later, they both still exuded the glamour, beauty and excitement that is synonymous with "stars".

"Command performances" were not a rarity at the Grove. As the Ambassador became internationally famous...as the logical hotel to host royalty...the night club became a must-see for them. Where earlier, you remember, the Grove had brought together "show-biz" people with old-guard society, now so was royalty eager to know these fascinating people.

Innumerable crowned heads of Europe and the Orient who have been lavishly entertained in the hotel and Grove include: Queen Wilhelmina of the Netherlands, later her daughter Queen Juliana and Prince Bernard, their Majesties, King Paul and Queen Frederika of Greece. The Crown Prince of Japan...was so taken with the "Cuban Fireball" Estrelita, appearing at that time, that after her performance, he ran into the lobby as she was leaving and asked for a dance. She replied, "Sorry, Prince, old boy, but my feet hurt!"

The Grove has been a stepping stone to fame for many of its performers. Bing Crosby became famous when he was heard coast to coast, and it triggered his own national radio program, and also led to movie assignments; Dean Martin got his first big picture break after an appearance, and it was the first big supper club to hire Harry Belafonte.

Others for whom the room was something of a magic amulet have been Pearl Bailey, Gordon MacRae and Dick Shawn. Barbra Streisand recalls that her three weeks at the Grove preceded her New York "Funny Girl" booking and success.

A local magazine reported, however, that it wasn't always lucky for everyone. "Yma Sumac collapsed during a performance...a doctor was summoned from the audience. Her problem wasn't serious, it seems she had consumed too much chili for her dinner.

"The Grove's policy", still reporting, "of photographic privacy for patrons unless they wish to be photographed, missed at least one of Hollywood's famous fights. The combatants were Dick Haymes and Rita Hayworth, and the winner was Haymes, at least to judge from Rita's black eye."

**Singer Dick Haymes between songs with his greatest fan, bride Rita Hayworth. Dancer/actress Rita became Mrs. Haymes after her divorce from Ali Khan and her experience as a princess.**

Similarly, May Mann, the very young and beautiful blond Hollywood reporter who was the darling of the stars, stepped out of her limousine bedecked in her finest evening attire. She was approached a few minutes later by an aide of a foreign dignitary asking for an introduction to be told, "Sorry, I'm late for an appointment in the Grove." The handsome man in the colorful and gold braided uniform who wished to meet her was the Shah of Iran!

Others were His Majesty King Faisal II of Iraq; Doctor Sukarno, President of Indonesia; President Celal Bayer of Turkey; and Emperor Haile Selassie I of Ethiopia. Of course, during these years, the Grove was honored to host U.S. Presidents, diplomats and dignitaries as well.

**Hollywood columnist and author, May Mann pretty enough to be in films herself, with handsome leading man George Hamilton.**

**Popular band leader Paul Neighbors shown with his big band when they played the Grove in the forties and fifties. Still fronting a big band, Neighbors plays the Texas, Louisiana, Kansas, and New York circuit. A drummer from age three, he's still at it.**

Dorothy Lamour guesting with the great Rudy Vallee. Starring with Don Ho during one of the Grove's last engagements in the seventies before the decor was changed, Dottie came on stage dressed in a sarong pulling a palm tree on rollers. The only one remaining, I have it in my office, monkey and all.

Another great drummer...Mickey Rooney, with Ann Rutherford.

"Jitterbugs" greeting Tommy Dorsay and Jack Arkin at the L.A. Railroad Depot...en route to the Grove.

# NAT KING COLE

## "Music, Music, Music"

**GROVE PERFORMERS**

Top left clockwise: Everybody's favorite, Nat King Cole, playing one of his records for Anna Kashfi and John Drew Barrymore, his co-stars on the MGM film NIGHT OF THE QUARTER MOON. Evenings would find the "king" entertaining at the Grove. Years later, his daughter Natalie would appear on the same stage as the featured singer.

Belafonte introduces his famous calypso style at the Grove.

Van Johnson drumming it up with June Allyson. Van starred in the "Music Man" musical comedy at the Grove. Probably the nation's first theatre supper club effort which is now so popular.

"Dino" . . . eating!

Grove musical favorites Kathryn Grayson and Howard Keel with beautiful and continental Zsa Zsa Gabor. Miss Gabor's jewels are as famous as is the actress, however she claims she wears only duplicates and locks up the real thing in her safe.

"Satchmo" Louis Armstrong and his trumpet were harbingers of peace around the world, long before it was considered necessary... with Grove Maitre'd Gilbert Paoli.

# the world famous
# cocoanut grove

The 50's and 60's featured many of the above while welcoming newcomers Diana Ross and The Supremes, the Fifth Dimension, and inviting back or introducing Tito Guizar, Lina Romay, Frank Fontaine, Yma Sumac, Wayne King, John Carroll, Patti Page, Andy and Della Russell. Estrelita, Alan King, Russ Morgan, Anne Jeffreys and Robert Sterling, the Jimmy McHugh show, Les Paul and Mary Ford, Toni Arden, Connie Russell, Paul Gilbert, Georgie Taps, Ames Brothers, the King Sisters, Kaye Ballard, The Sportsmen, Xavier Cugat and Abbe Lane, Ted Lewis, Gale Storm, Dick Contino, Jane Froman, Carol Channing, Patrice Wymore, Eartha Kitt, Eydie Gorme, Jaye P. Morgan, Teresa Brewer, George Gobel, Dennis Day, Shirley Jones, Nelson Eddy, Johnny, Brascia & Tybee, The Kingston Trio, Phil Ford and Mimi Hines, Vivienne Della Chiesa, Allen & Rossi, Tommy Sands, Gogi Grant, Rowan & Martin, Buddy Hackett, Jack Jones, Polly Bergen, Tony Sandler & Ralph Young, Buddy Greco, Wayne Newton, Kaye Stevens, Wiere Brothers, Phyllis Diller, Don Ho, Petula Clark, Brenda Lee, the Righteous Brothers, Al Martino, Larry Storch, George Carlin, Lana Cantrall, John Gary, Lou Rawls, Shirley Bassey, Ella Fitzgerald, Mrs. Miller, Bobby Vinton, Connie Francis, the Kim Sisters, Miriam Makeba, Ray Charles, Keefe Braselle, Alice Lon, Bill Bendix, Bernie Richards, Ken Murray, Johnny Mathis, the June Taylor dancers, Corbett Monica, Jack Carter, Milton Berle, Giselle MacKenzie, Joni James, Pearl Bailey, Myron Cohen, Dennis Morgan, Paul Anka, Della Reese, Dave Barry, Georgia Gibbs, Pat Boone, Louis Prima & Keely Smith, Frank Gorshin, Will Mastin Trio, Joe E. Lewis...all the greatest.

Guy Lombardo's remark was widely quoted, "A bid to play *the* room on the West Coast, has always been like a command performance before royalty. And it was always desirable because it was practically a guarantee that we could do film work during the day, then have the great exposure of the Grove coast to coast broadcasts in the evening... a sure thing to fame and fortune for singers and musicians."

Pat Henry, Louis Armstrong, Donald O'Connor, Jackie Mason, Vince Edwards, The Johnny Mann Singers, Robert Goulet, Kay Starr, Juliet Prowse, Carol Lawrence, Les Brown, Nancy Wilson, Eddie Bergman Strings, The Stingers, Leslie Uggams, Roberta Sherwood, the George Shearing Quintet, The Four Freshmen, Count Basie, Barbara McNair, Vikki Carr, Diahann Carroll were regulars.

**Dynamite singing star Barbra Streisand gained wide attention while starring at the Grove in 1963. Shown with her then-husband Elliott Gould who later was an Ambassador neighbor, living at the nearby Windsor Hotel.**

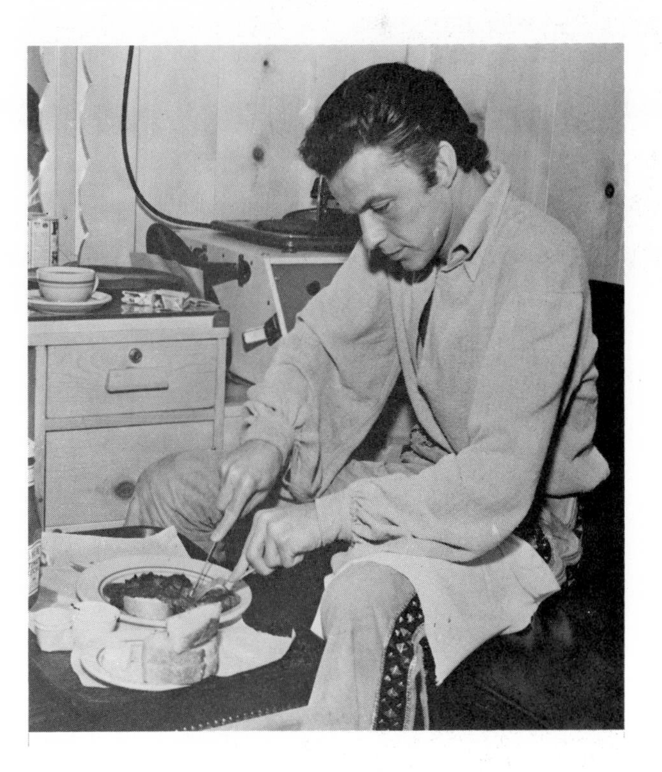

**"Blue Eyes" Sinatra dining backstage. Alone?**

Singing star Tony Martin appearing at the Grove.

In 1957, David Schine, president of Schine Enterprises who then owned the Ambassador Hotel, welcomed preview guests to the new modernized Grove which had cost more than $750,000. He said, "It was a delicate task to redo a room with so many traditions and so many fond memories and to bring to it the glamour and excitement befitting this dynamic heart-center of show business.

"We dedicate ourselves to perpetuating its great tradition," he said.

Newspapers noted that California's Governor and Mrs. Knight headed up the list of dignitaries which included leaders of the social, business and political world. Those from the Hollywood film colony included Gary Cooper, Fred Astaire, Sophia Loren, Jayne Mansfield, Groucho Marx, Jack Lemmon, Richard Egan, Ernie Kovacs, Arthur O'Connell, Katherine Grayson, Mae Murray, Francis X. Bushman and Leo Carrillo.

"And a new era began last night at the Cocoanut Grove. The world-famed Ambassador supper club, a Los Angeles after-dark institution for nearly four decades," reported the Los Angeles Times, "became a new being with a new look, a new smile on its face, and a new, jaunty tilt to its top hat. Friends came to ring in the new...and ring out the old.

"They found much that was familiar ..and much that had been changed. The famed cocoanut palms that gave this hotel oasis its name still leaned above them against an azure sky. The rococo Moorish brilliance that had always been a tradition with the room...the scarlet, gold and black...was retained but altered toward the modern manner.

David Schine surveying the modernization of the Cocoanut Grove.

Silent screen star Mae Murray of the bee stung lips with California Governor Goodwin Knight.

ɔmantic silent screen star ancis X. Bushman . . . th his real life wife.

"Many were present who had been coming to the Grove for various celebrations for more than 30 years. Mae Murray found her 25 year old autograph on a treasured violin. Francis X. Bushman, a matinee idol when the Grove first opened attended on that occasion and was present to view the changes. Jesse L. Lasky, the movie pioneer who once judged dance contests on the floor, came to judge the changes.

"Many who came to remember the Grove as it once was...watched as their grandchildren danced."

Of the renovation, Los Angeles Times Society Columnist Christy Fox wrote "All over Our Town, chatting with people at parties, on the telephone and reading many letters, the question has nothing to do with charity, sports events or even spectaculars. It is the nostalgic feeling of people in our great city about something that 'belongs'...the world-famous Cocoanut Grove of the Ambassador.

"Probably the most beloved public room of all time, the Grove is wrapped up in the lives and loves of so many Angelenos that its fate is like learning about someone in the family. The minute news leaked out that the Grove was to be redecorated, the questions began..."Will they keep the old palm trees? How about the waterfall?"

"My husband proposed to me in the Grove"..."We always went on Friday nights when we were in college"..."How about the old Turf and Field Club"...Remember the Twenty Little Working Girls?...

"Here are the answers: The Cocoanut Grove will open with the Martins (Tony and Freddie) who will take over both vocally and instrumentally.

"The Grove has been brought up to date, but the "Feel" of the wonderful old room remains.

"What makes this news? Because the people, you and I...who have loved the Grove for many years, really and truly care.

"I'll never forget my first glimpse of the room...a fantasy of a palace. When it was opened it was hailed as a tribute to a city which had 'arrived'. Names like S.W. Straus, J.E. Benton, Ben Frank, and J. Myer Schine have had a strong hand in its shaping through the years, as have Jimmy Manus, Reuben Arvanoff and Michael Chumo, Gus Lampe and Uno Timanson, Grove Maitre d's and managers through the years."

Christy said, "The room is world-renowned, but in the hearts of so many who have danced and romanced there over the years, it is *the* place."

The sixties slipped away with the conservative style entertainment of Frankie Laine, Phyllis Newman, Morgana King, Victor Borge, Howard Keel with Kathryn Grayson, and the Lennon Sisters.

But as times, conditions, styles, modes and moods change so did the Grove.

Director Mervyn Le Roy on stage with the Dancing Champions.

The curtain fell on both Gower Champion and the successful opening of his latest Broadway show 42ND STREET on the same night. The popular dancer, choreographer, actor, director and showman died at the age of 61 of a rare blood disease. His brilliant show business career was launched when he won a Major Bowes contest in the Cocoanut Grove. dancing with his young high school partner Marge, who was to become his wife.

Sammy Davis Jr. explaining the anticipated "Now Grove" renovation to take place following a wrecking party. Guests were invited to tear down drapes, palm trees and interior decor, which many treasured as souvenirs. Many felt it was an "infamous" assault on the celebrated room, however with the new SUPERSTAR policy, the Grove jumped, sparkled and grooved.

Big business had fallen off in night clubs all over the nation...and the Grove was also a victim to the waning interest in big bands and "proper" kinds of nights out. But close the Grove? Revenue was down, but the Grove was a Los Angeles tradition, so management, under the guidance of then president Hugh Wiley opted to redesign the room and bring it up to date.

They would attract and pay the astronomical prices of the "superstars" attempting to duplicate the success of Las Vegas policy. With the advice of stellar star Sammy Davis (who was to reopen the room...his first appearance being years before as a member of the Will Mastin Trio), in the areas of decor, sound and lighting, the room was gutted and rebuilt adding more tables and seats. A totally new look was created. Sammy's was a personal crusade to maintain the nightclub for Los Angeles. Again performers were attracted by the same early interest "playing the Grove" elicited. It provided an opportunity for stars to stay in their California homes...near Hollywood where they could also book work in films with the added advantage of television.

Entertainment writer John Scott reported, "An invitational audience broke more than glasses at the Grove's 'Wrecking Party' preceding the official renovation. One fabulous era has ended. But hopefully, another begins."

Scott ended his story there...but many Angeleno's hearts were broken to see 'their' cherished room destroyed, nay, profaned .

Grove interior under reconstruction with less than two weeks remaining before scheduled opening. Under the direction of foreman Gregorian, work continued around the clock.

Sammy "sidewalk superintending" with Governor Nigh and friends.

Mrs. Sammy Davis with Ross Martin.
Paul and Dorothy Neighbors.
Mr. and Mrs. Henry Mancini.
**George Kennedy and another guest.**

Diana Ross . . . in hot-hot pants.
Joey Bishop, Edward G. Robinson
and Toni Holt.

Hugh Wiley and Robert Culp.
Edward G. Robinson and Mia Farrow.
MOD SQUAD's Clarence Williams and his wife.
Mr. and Mrs. Sugar Ray Robinson.

Visions of the new Grove. Again, Grove fans everywhere were avidly watching developments

A survey determining to keep the room open had concluded that (1) people genuinely regarded Los Angeles as the entertainment capitol of the world and expected top live entertainment when they visited that city, (2) surprisingly, over 70% of the audience were residents, rather than tourists, (3) and that the Cocoanut Grove was still revered as the world's greatest nightclub by people everywhere.

In April of 1970, George Rhodes' band, kleig lights and hundreds of revelers welcomed Sammy Davis who arrived by slick motorcycle in a sparkling, bejeweled costume to herald opening night of the "Now" Grove...in startling contrast to the top-hat and tails audience who had been there for the same purpose exactly 49 years earlier.

Designed by Phyllis Mann and Harry Fox, seating arrangements were increased, and startling colors of black, silver, purple, orange, pinks and black were used. The interior boasted a circular effect with lamps in the ceiling where the stars had been, and illuminated railings separated the various rises. A huge glassed-in cocktail court (where an open, romantic balcony had offered a view of the stars, sky and city to dancers years before), and new Wilshire Boulevard entrance surrounded double curving stairways, and a sparkling gargantuan chandelier shone out into the night.

Spiffy new high-rise sign which could be seen for miles. Gone was the classical pylon and statue of Betty Grable. No more could the college kids fill the fountain with soap for the suds to foam down Wilshire Boulevard.

Hugh Wiley and fans greeting Sammy Davis on opening night.

# "Another Opening, Another Show"

Voila . . . another opening . . .
Suzanne Pleshette and her "real" husband Tommy Gallagher.
Fred Williamson and Brenda Sykes.

Once again, opening night audiences were star-studded. Elbow to elbow with people great and small could be found: Robert Stack, Steve Allen, Pat Boone, Jackie Cooper, Glenn Ford, George Burns, George Hamilton, Jack Lemmon, Ricardo Montalban, Lee Majors, Johnny Mathis, Raquel Welch, Flip Wilson, David Janssen, Kirk Douglas, Gene Kelly, Donald O'Connor, Red Skelton, Ross Hunter, Jan Murray, Ken Murray, Jimmie Stewart, Dinah Shore, Edith Head, Lana Turner, Andy Williams, Sugar Ray Robinson, Robert Wagner, Natalie Wood...and their respective husbands, wives, girl and boy friends.

Everybody's favorite George Burns.
Art Metrano and Madelyn Rhue.
Jack Hyde and Flip Wilson.

Margaret, orchestra leader Orrin and Mrs. Tucker and Superior Judge James Tante.

Assemblyman and Mrs. Charles Warren, Judge and Mrs. Tante, and Shirley Hufstedler. Since this photo, Warren and Justice Hufstedler have been appointed to important posts in the nation's capitol.

Ike Jones and Barbara McNair.
Liza Minnelli with Robert and Rosemary Stack.

Beaded gowns and chiffon mingled with unshirted leather vested and weird "way-out" costumes of the day, and enthusiasm was high as Sammy's versatile and talent-packed act followed an epicurean feast accompanied by strolling violinists.

And the paparazzi were in full force, guaranteeing photos of the Grove and its cast of revelers appearing in newspapers and magazines all over the world.

Mr. and Mrs. Fred Falcone (Justice Mildred Lillie).

Taking its cue from Las Vegas, the Grove booked "super-stars" and Los Angeles revelled in its exciting and sophisticated top entertainment.Consensus of opinion was that the Grove also "looked" Las Vegas.

All of the entertainment world's stellar lights were engaged. Sonny & Cher, Liza Minelli, Duke Ellington, Sarah Vaughn, Dionne Warwick, Diana Ross, Sergio Franchi, Aretha Franklin, Pearl Bailey and Louis Belson, Billy Eckstine, Tony Bennett, Ella Fitzgerald, Count Basie, Nancy Sinatra, Debbie Reynolds, Frank Gorshin & Pat Paulsen, Temptations & Supremes, Connie Stevens, Jack Jones, Phyllis Diller, Buck Owens, the King Family, Ray Charles, the Burgundy Street Singers, Dick Haymes, Juliet Prowse, David Brenner...with Sammy making frequent appearances.

Nancy Sinatra receiving her official opening night bouquet. Columnists were all but making book on whether father Frank would be at his reserved table for Nancy's show as officials were trying to serve him with a subpoena to testify in regards to his gambling casino affiliations. We all missed him . . . but his was no doubt the greatest disappointment.

"The Schnozz" with his pals. Following Jimmy Durante's show, Danny Thomas and Joey Bishop joined Jimmy, Eddie Jackson and Sonny King for the usual opening night "roast."

Juliet Prowse gave her usual hard-driving, spectacular performance . . .from two stages . . . in spite of her 5 month pregnancy. Even if Juliet wasn't nervous . . . her audience was!

"Pearlie May" Bailey.
Diana Ross.
The Supremes.

Rouvan as Pagliacci.
Lester and Willy Tyler.
Billy Eckstine.

Another second generation performer . . . Nancy Sinatra, whose Dad made the Grove long before she did.

The Grove's entertainment program was a tremendous success, audiences loved the acts, music and wonderful evenings provided for them...but much of the time expenses exceeded revenue, which prompted longer dark periods between acts in the few years that followed.

The Mills Brothers . . . world-favorites for over 50 years.
Ray Charles . . . with feeling.
Second generation. . . Liza singing her heart out as her mother Judy Garland did before her.

# Great Grove Moments

(On right) The Incomparable Lena Horne.

There have been so many great moments in the Grove . . . these are a few: After a great Sammy Davis rendition of a selection from the "Music Man," the singer was heckled by a man in the audience. Several times Sammy was interrupted while trying to announce his next song, and he remained polite, but was getting annoyed. Finally, the heckler said Sammy's was the best he had ever heard, and "why don't you ask me who I am?" Sammy did, and the answer was, "Meredith Willson"! Sammy invited the famed composer up to the stage, and together they thrilled the audience with "76 Trombones."

Staunchly supported on her "return" to show business, Judy Garland, with Tony Bennett.

Don Ho being greeted by Roger Carroll when he arrived for his engagement at the Grove. Ho's totally new, breezy style attracted young people who eagerly "hulued" on stage at Ho's invitation.

A resident when in town making pictures, Maurice Chevalier, who could usually be persuaded to sing his "Louise."

Ella Fitzgerald . . . a real trouper. Ella wouldn't miss a performance even though she had eye surgery a few days before. The lights were mercilessly bright, but sing she did, with her eyes closed.

A successful opening night for Bobby Darin. A short while later he was gone . . .victim to a heart condition.

Anthony Newley, "the entertainers' entertainer."

# "Just One More Chance"

"JUST ONE MORE CHANCE"
**Jerry Johnson, Jimmy Henderson and John Mace.**

"Cocoanut" once more replaced "Now" by then manager John Mace and entrepreneur Jerry Johnson. Calling the entertainment "Sight and Sound", the room featured Beverly Bremer, Jeremy Vernon, Skiles & Henderson, Jerry Van Dyke, Kay Ballard, the Sylvers, the Four Tops, Freda Payne, Gloria Loring and Stanley Myron Handelman, and many other performers who worked for less than the staggering salaries demanded by so called "superstars".

Why would name stars agree to these conditions? According to headlining Kay Ballard, and some of the others, said Jerry Johnson, "They realize that nightclubs must be preserved or soon there will be no place for stars to work. It has been our hope that the greats of show business would respect their obligation to put something back into the business from which they have been prospering for many years. We believe that Kay's and other's willingness to cooperate will turn the tide to preserve the Cocoanut Grove for future generations. We are paying what we can afford, and the stars who cooperate with this internationally famous nightclub not only enhance their own career credits, but also have the advantage of a well equipped stage and magnificent orchestra to sharpen their repertoire and break in new material. Also it provides that they do not have to work consistently in a gambling environment (Las Vegas)."

Adding to the fun and frivolity were the "Cocoanuts", a line of fast dancing and gorgeous girls who appeared with every show. And Jimmy Henderson provided beautiful big band sounds for the dancing that had helped to make the Grove famous.

And personable host, the well-known maitre'd of the Grove for many years, Gilbert Paoli, continued to greet his many fans.

Of the opening on Halloween night, 1972, reporter Beverly Sue wrote, "Anyone reaching the ripe age of 51 must have a few tell-tale lines on his face and maybe an extra bulge or two.

"Not so with the Cocoanut Grove. The famous old supper-club, looks like a youngster. The most efficient beauty experts in the world, the staff of the Ambassador Hotel have kept the room and the entire hostelry for that matter, 'Younger than Springtime'.

"The Cocoanut Grove and Hollywood's fabled moving picture industry are so intertwined that at times it's difficult to tell one from the other. All the movie greats came to the Cocoanut Grove, as well as Los Angeles society since its birth...and they're still coming."

**Los Angeles' friend, Council President John Ferraro and Jerry Johnson.**

Grove Maitre'd Gilbert Paoli, singer Gloria Loring, George Salomonides and Rudy Vallee.

Myron Handleman and the Mills Brothers.

Jan Murray.

Jack Carter and Patti Andrews.

A soloing Ames Brother, Ed.

Frank Duvall, Paoli and Singing Jack Smith.

Ernest Borgnine and Marty Allen.

Singer Vic Damone entertaining actress Danielle Darrieux his co-star in RICH, YOUNG AND PRETTY, during his engagement at the Grove.

Los Angeles' winningest team, Lohman and Barclay from KFI deciding where to hang their poster prior to their Grove engagement. Civic minded duo is always ready to answer calls to aid worthwhile projects.

But again, expenses and lack of support for night clubs joined forces with a national economic recession to stall the activities for a period.

But interest has always been keen in the Grove, and once again it opened to "Concerts at the Grove", a theme started by well known jazz entrepreneur Howard Rumsey and jazz aficionado and enthusiast Milt Handman with plans geared primarily toward jazz orchestras, combos and singers.

Featured were Ike and Tina Turner with their Revue, Dizzy Gillespie, Carmen McRae, Morganna King, Esther Phillips, Natalie Cole and Hubert Laws.

Theatre in the Round, Ram's Games Sunday Dances, and even opera with "Lucia De Lammermoor" presented by the American Theatre of the Opera appeared in the Grove. Add to that fashion shows and exotic presentations, such as a contest for the "Queen" of female impersonators!

Presently, the Grove is used for private parties, gala affairs, filmings and specials...many booked by people who have happy memories of the exciting times they had in the room that is a continuing legend.

And Freddy Martin still comes back to play for dancers on New Year's Eve, sometimes.

Doris Day first
-nighting. As a
band singer with
Les Brown, Doris had
appeared in the Grove.

Peggy Lee, now
headlining, was once
the vocalist with
Benny Goodman.

Kim Novak, Shirley MacLaine on the town
with Ernie Kovacs..
Oh-so-beautiful Elizabeth Taylor and husband
Michael Wilding.

## "Are The Stars Out Tonight?"

Since opening night, the Cocoanut Grove refrain has always been, "Are the stars out tonight?"

They came to entertain and to be entertained...and the public came to see the stars...and to be entertained.

On stage, and in the audience...as the fan magazines put it..."More stars than in the sky"...

Clockwise from the top:
Stars sharing bon mots and secrets . . . with columnist Hedda Hopper wishing the walls could talk. Popular once-married duo, Tony Curtis and Janet Leigh. Anthony Quinn congratulating Totie Fields on opening night. Humphrey Bogart giving Marlene Dietrich his full attention; Elia Kazan listening in. Hedda. Handsome Robert Taylor and his wife Ursula Thiess with headlining Anna Maria Alberghetti.

## "If Only The Walls Could Talk"

Jane Wyman telling it like it is, Ginger Rogers with Mr. and Mrs. Alan Ladd, Mrs. Ladd with a little Ladd. Bing Crosby, returning to the scene of his success (after many years' absence. Crosby had been fired from the Grove after his spectacular success there, and vowed never to return), Mr. and Mrs. Jackie Cooper and Mr. and Mrs.Jack Oakie.

Left column: "Who's kidding who?. . .comedians Frank Gorshin, Tommy Smothers and Red Buttons. Jimmy Durante, Edward G. Robinson, B'nai B'rith Messenger Publisher Gil Thompson and Mrs. Thompson. The popular Robert Stacks.

Center column: Harry Burk, Saundra Zagaria, Lola Falana and friends with Debbie Reynolds following the star's opening. Debby had as her guests the entire retirement home where her father resided. Resident Jimmy McHugh and entertainer/businesswoman Polly Bergen. Star paying homage to a star is Johnny Mathis greeting Dick Haymes on opening night with Mrs. Dick Haymes and "Batman" Adam West. Haymes was as good as ever, even though he had just returned from several years of self-exile in Europe.

Right column: Wayne Newton, the Robert Weisses and Variety's Tony Scott. Ever-loving Jimmy again with Alaska's Senator Mike Gravel, Meredith News Chain Entertainment Editor Fil Perell and Jimmy's little Margie.

## "Join The Party"

"Sensational", "Terrific", "Great show", "Better than ever", "A hit"...is champagne, milk and honey, sweet perfume and the next thing to Heaven to every performer.

And that's the tenor and tone of the after-show reception for first nighters, friends and other entertainers as they greet the STAR of the night.

# Sunshine And Shadows

In Hollywood one could shoot pirates on a South Sea Beach; track dusty, dishelved Foreign Legionnaires as they marched across Sahara sands; observe Hannibal as he scaled the Alps; and ride a wild horse to cut the bad bandidos off at the pass. You could wildly careen across a busy horse and wagon intersection in a Model-T driven by cross-eyed Ben Turpin; to be chased by the Keystone Kops; or stand trembling below Harold Lloyd as he hangs from the hands of a clock 3 stories atop a building. Or perhaps eat and drink heartily at a gluttonous table while watching Rome burn; later to be seduced by a vampire in a flowing silk robe, or a red-hot vamp in a beaded one.

And get paid for it.

Sunshine had been the siren's call to the moviemakers, and they trekked to Southern California. And the mountains, natural light, mild climate and long days created the Hollywood that became the film capitol of the world.

It was one of the few things that happened to Southern California spontaneously. No booster program drew this industry, nor could even the greatest visionaries or city-planners foresee the magical growth of Hollywood Movieland.

David and William Horsley came from New Jersey with their Nestor Film Company and started the Hollywood of Today shooting a "Western" in the old Blondeau barn which doubled as a studio. The natives were actually frightened when they saw heavily armed cowboys galloping up Beachwood Drive to "fight" Indians that they thought had left long ago...

I Love You California

Mary Garden stopped Grand Opera to make this California song famous

Motion picture companies were not entirely unknown in Los Angeles when Hollywood was "discovered" as the future cinema capital.

As early as 1904 a film had been shot in old Chutes Park of Roy Knabenshue's dirigible.

1907 saw the first movie to be made in Hollywood (in a tavern and barn at the corner of Sunset Boulevard and Gower Street) and in the same year, because of the influx of inhabitants and the town's need for additional water, Hollywood was consolidated with Los Angeles.

Then Colonel Selig rented a boom-time mansion at Eighth and Olive early in 1908 and made "In the Sultan's Power". It was the first complete motion picture made in Los Angeles.

In 1909 The New York Motion Picture Company sent the old Bison Company to Hollywood. It turned out a "Western" every day and a half. In January, 1910, came the Biograph Company and D.W. Griffith. With him and unknown to fame at that time were Mack Sennett, Owen Moore and Mary Pickford. Mary Pickford had started the year before in pictures at $5.00 a day. In 1910, Essany, and then Kalem came to the Coast.

Lasky, with Cecil B. De Mille and Dustin Farnum as director and star respectively, ventured to Hollywood in 1913 and, renting a barn across from an orange orchard, made the "Squaw Man". Unlike Nestor, which had refused to buy five acres around their barn at $4,000 because they had been warned to "beware of California real estate agents," Lasky purchased acreage around his stable and built a permanent studio. Today the property is valuable beyond estimation.

De Mille, in his famous jodphurs and boots would ride horseback from the studio across the vast plains of the Cahuenga Pass to his home. One sunset he experienced highwaymen's rifle shots aimed at him, but escaped their gun fire. A scenario as exciting as in any of his films.

Before 1913 had passed, Mary Pickford had made "Tess of the Storm Country" for $1,000 a week and Griffith, originator of the "switch back", the "fadeout" and "sustained suspense", was filming "The Birth of a Nation", using for the first time extras numbering into the thousands. At that time, before unions, the whole town would turn up at the studio to work as extras.

When the picture had its premiere at the Philharmonic Auditorium in 1915, overnight successes were Mae Marsh, Lillian Gish and Donald Crisp. The fame of this picture has seldom been equalled. It is still a major attraction, and it helped in making Los Angeles the foremost, the permanent and recognized seat of the modern picture industry.

An observer was soon to write, "The legendary Hollywood is a sort of Venice without canals, full of glittering conveyances, dazzling maidens, and god-like men...marble swimming pools abound and champagne flows everywhere."

Then came Charlie Chaplin, leaving a traveling troupe of English pantomimists to go to work on the Keystone lot for $150 a week. Two years later found him receiving $10,000 a week and he was the most widely visualized personality in the history of the world.

Fox introduced demure and prudent Theodosia Goodman, who as Theda Bara became the first motion picture "vamp". By 1914 Lasky was paying Mary Pickford so much she could no longer make one-reelers. By 1916, she had signed her name to a million-dollar contract. Bill Hart, Douglas Fairbanks, and Constance Talmadge were claiming their fame, and Anita Loos, a San Diego High School girl, was paid $15 for writing a scenario, and was urged to write more...and more she is still writing, while in her nineties. One of Anita's best known books was "Gentlemen Prefer Blondes". A great influence on her beautiful niece, Mary Loos, who, like Anita preferred writing to acting, has just completed her fourth successful book on Hollywood.

By 1917, First National had taken Pickford and Chaplin away at even greater figures and the latter had brought Jackie Coogan, a small boy who had winked at him in a Los Angeles railway station, to fame and fortune in "The Kid."

Jackie Coogan greeting Charlie Chaplin nearly 60 years after the foremost comedian discovered that little boy.

World War I intervened, the studios turned out patriotic films to boost morale, and many stars, headed up by Douglas Fairbanks, Mary Pickford, Charlie Chaplin and Marie Dressler made personal appearances all over the country to sell war bonds.

Superstars of the 20's were Swanson, Pickford, Fairbanks, Chaplin, Lon Chaney, Tom Mix, the Gish sisters, Harold Lloyd, Pola Negri and the Talmadge sisters, Norma and Constance.

Rudolph Valentino became the heart throb of a nation, only to be dead a few scant years later. The quixotic Italian landscape gardener flamed across the firmament as a love symbol. He had become a millionaire, but his money couldn't solve his dilemmas of romance or health. Quickly "copies" were developed in the forms of Ricardo Cortez, Antonio Moreno, Ramon Navarro and Gilbert Roland.

Director William Desmond Taylor was mysteriously murdered, and his lady friends Mabel Normand and Mary Minter (and her mother) were under suspicion, which ruined their acting careers. Screen comedian Fatty Arbuckle was implicated in the death of starlet Virginia Rappe who died of sexual perversions at an orgy, and concluded his successful film-making.

Great excesses of money, easy access to bootleg booze and narcotics led to the ends of careers, death and sometimes suicide of rising young stars.

The screen's All-American Boy Wallace Reid was hooked on morphine. Like all famous addicts, he was bled dry by blackmailers...to die from an overdose.

The California State Board of Pharmacy revealed it had more than 500 prominent movie people listed as drug addicts.

The "Hollywoodland" sign was built on a hill for everyone to see. The thrills it has provided for the thousands of hopefuls that made it to the film capital would be hard to estimate. A few unsuccessful aspirants used the sign from which to plunge to their deaths.

American mores and morals changed rapidly in the 20th Century. The war had ended and people realized that life could be short...many young men had finished theirs on foreign shores...so that decade "roared"; dresses rose above the knees; boys became "sheiks"; flasks smuggled rot-gut gin; life was the "cat's pajamas" and jazz was its tempo.

Now that the industry was in Hollywood to stay, actors, who in the roving old days had no chance to take root, build a home or care for property, to raise and educate children, to take part in civic affairs or in any kind of normal life, could now settle down and live a respectable existence and do all of those things.

The Ambassador took her place in the life and family of the movie colony. It was the meeting place of the stars. Business meetings, parties, balls, banquets and living facilities were always at the ready. Weddings, dances and tete-a-tetes were held at the fashionable, rambling and beautiful hotel, and many of the new arrivals from the New York theatre were escorted to the "in" place as an indication of their importance.

So the fledgling motion picture business, the city and the brand new hotel, grew together, nurtured each other and flourished.

Gloria Swanson lived in one of the bungalows soon after the hotel opened with her husband Herb Somborn, owner of the Brown Derby directly across the boulevard. In Siesta bungalow were John Barrymore, Zelda and Scott Fitzgerald, famous author Joe Hergesheimer, and intermittantly Carmel Myers. Rudolph Valentino and Pola Negri were just next door.

Other residents were Jetta Goudal, Clara Bow, Marion Davies and William Randolph Hearst...together and simultaneously, they were building Hollywood and her legends.

It was an extravagant time...entertainment became lavish...and films demonstrated the lush, loose and daring life. Movie "temples" featured spectacles, but then there were also the "Ben-Hurs", "The Ten Commandments", and "The Covered Wagon". These were the "glory" years of the silent screen, and sound and technicolor were on their way.

But as with any sudden explosion of wealth or success, as in a gold rush or oil strike, the first flush of craziness, opulence, spending and high-living of the newly discovered film business settled back into the pattern of living and working.

And it was about this time that the industry recognized itself as an emphatic, if sometimes imprudent force on the life-styles and philosophies of the entire world.

Enter the Academy Awards.

**Bridal shower for Gloria Swanson (L to R) Yvonne Skelton, Claire Windsor, Marion Davies, Gloria Swanson, Constance Talmadge, Adela Rogers St. Johns and Louella Parsons.**

Exotic early star, Jetta Goudal.

Carmel Myers in a torrid love scene with Francis X. Bushman.

# "Oscar Doesn't Live Here Anymore"

It was a sell-out. Every seat was occupied with chattering, excited, hopeful and apprehensive people. Mostly actors, producers, directors and technicians in the motion picture business comprised the audience.

It was awards night, when the industry saluted its own...and gave recognition to the best among them.

Suddenly, the lights went out. The huge, cavernous Grove became a deep well of black velvet. Just as suddenly, chattering stopped mid-sentence, the orchestra halted mid-note and in the darkness hands groped for one another. Frightening to some..."oh hell, the power is off" to others.

When the stealth and quiet was total, a pin point of light needled its way from the ceiling through the black, coming to rest on a single shimmering gold figure which was waiting alone on the stage...waiting to be introduced.

It was "Oscar"...who at that moment became the symbol that each and every person connected with the industry would wish for...strive for, and compete for from that moment on. For Oscar represented the Best, and would bring with it recognition, honor and riches...from the whole world.

The excitement and pride in winning the coveted award for best films, performances and creative and technical achievements is shared by fans and movie buffs wherever movies are shown.

Mary Pickford and Warner Baxter receiving their awards from the Academy of Motion Picture Arts and Sciences ... Mr. "Oscar."

Norma Shearer with her coveted fellow.

Bette Davis, a two-time Academy winner, holds a near record of 10 nominations in the field of acting and is a past president of the Academy of Motion Picture Arts and Sciences. Of the awards, she said, "For all the members of the Academy, an Oscar is the highest and most cherished of honors in a world where many honors are bestowed annually. It has become an incentive for better work and subconsciously is a goal toward which many members of the motion picture industry strive all year".

Oscar was born at one of the most crucial junctures in American history, just months before the stock market crash would send the country reeling into a decade-long Great Depression. Hollywood too, was experiencing its greatest crisis. Silent Movies collapsed with the birth of "Talkies".

The Academy Award trophy, "Oscar" first saw the light of day in the Cocoanut Grove of the Ambassador Hotel on April 3, 1930. It was the third awards celebration, but the first to present the gold statuette. It was also the first of six Academy banquets to be held at the Ambassador, and the last where a dinner was served, to be succeeded by a move to larger arenas beginning with Grauman's Chinese Theatre, and more lately the Music Center.

All of the films nominated the first year were silents. None of the films nominated the second year were. Sound had arrived.

MGM mogul L.B. Mayer, winner Helen Hayes and thespian Lionel Barrymore.

Walt Disney and Shirley Temple "surrounded."

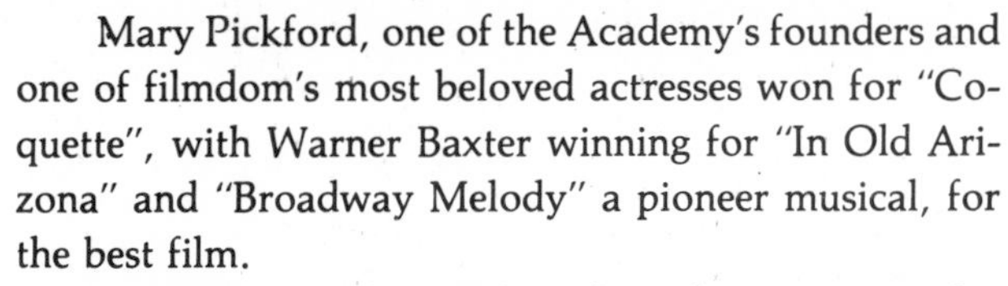

Mary Pickford, one of the Academy's founders and one of filmdom's most beloved actresses won for "Coquette", with Warner Baxter winning for "In Old Arizona" and "Broadway Melody" a pioneer musical, for the best film.

Los Angeles radio KFI broadcast the ceremonies for the first time.

In 1931 the desire to win an Oscar became fierce. Norma Shearer beat out Greta Garbo and Gloria Swanson. Other winners were George Arliss and "All Quiet on the Western Front". Thomas Edison spoke to the members as they were assembled in the Grove.

In 1933 Franklin Delano Roosevelt had just been elected President in a landslide. Eight days later the Academy Awards were presented in the Grove with Lionel Barrymore as M.C., and Helen Hayes was named best actress. "Grand Hotel" won for picture of the year, and Wallace Beery in "The Champ" tied with Frederic March for "Dr. Jekyll and Mr. Hyde". By coincidence, both actors had adopted children shortly before.

"It seems a little odd," said March in his acceptance speech, "That Beery and I were given awards for the best male performance of the year!"

A special award went to Walt Disney...he was the father of a mouse, called Mickey.

Katherine Hepburn did not appear to accept her award in 1934, but nonetheless for her role in "Morning Glory" she was heralded as a great discovery. Miss Hepburn didn't make an Academy appearance until almost 40 years later. "Cavalcade" was the best picture, and Charles Laughton best actor. Will Rogers was the M.C. and he called the ceremony "the last roundup of the ermine in the Grove Corral."

Talented trio, Laurel and Hardy surrounding Walt.

GONE WITH THE WIND. . . winners, Vivien Leigh and Olivia de Havilland with Miss Leigh's husband English actor Lawrence Olivier.

Never did the Awards ceremonies create more excitement than in 1940 when "Gone With the Wind" swept most of the awards, especially for best picture, and Vivien Leigh, English newcomer for best actress for her portrayal of Scarlet in the film which also starred Clark Gable who, along with nominee Jimmy Stewart for "Mr. Smith Goes to Washington" lost to Robert Donat for "Goodbye, Mr. Chips".

Quotes from newspapers of that day reported that Bette Davis applauded happily when Vivien Leigh won for the role that she "wanted mightily...along with every other actress in Hollywood".

Judy and Mickey.

Hattie McDaniel . . . a garden of gardenias.

"Crowds lined up in front of the Ambassador went wild as their favorites, Gary Cooper, Claudette Colbert, Robert Taylor, Barbara Stanwyck, Myrna Loy, Gable, Lombard, Olivia De Havilland, Spencer Tracy among all the rest of the screen's stellar lights arrived. Vivien Leigh arriving with producer Selznick nearly caused a riot as a mob of fans rushed forward," wrote Hedda Hopper the Hollywood scribe.

"Even royalty hasn't such difficulty seating their crowned heads. Everybody was there." Speakers were Frank Capra, Walter Wanger, Bob Benchley, Darryl Zanuck, Frank Freeman, Mervyn Le Roy, Jimmy Roosevelt, Sinclair Lewis, Spencer Tracy and Fay Bainter. Young Doug accepted a statuette in honor of his late father, Douglas Fairbanks, and Norma Shearer, the beautiful widow of Irving Thalberg for his ideals and courage in the industry.

Mickey Rooney, the year's previous juvenile winner presented a trophy to 17-year old Judy Garland, and she sang the year's "best song", "Over the Rainbow", accompanied by Guy Lombardo and his orchestra.

Supporting actress in GWTW Hattie McDaniel became the first Negro to win an Oscar. "With a wide grin, six gardenias in her hair and a green velvet sash around her ample middle, she was the hit of the evening", said Hedda.

Producer David Selznick with a stunning portrait of his star "Scarlett."

Honor guests from all branches of the service were in attendance at the 1943 ceremonies as Hollywood and America was well into the second World War. Louella Parsons recounted, "The most thrilling event of the banquet at the Ambassador was the unfurling of the American flag with 27,677 names of members of the motion picture industry who are in uniform answering Uncle Sam's call. Tyrone Power was handsome in his Marine dress uniform, Alan Ladd dignified in his Army khakis.

"With Bob Hope as M.C., messages were read from Madame Chiang Kai-Shek and President Roosevelt, and Jeanette MacDonald sang the National Anthem. Van Heflin, a new Lieutenant in the Air Force was in uniform to accept his supporting actor plaque, thanking the Army for 'letting him off'. Margaret Wyler got a big hand when she thanked the Academy for Willie's prize and said it meant so much to him who is overseas now, a Major in the Army. Ronald Colman was a great sport and hurried to congratulate Jimmy Cagney for his "Yankee Doodle Dandy" best actor award, not showing his own disappointment. Irving Berlin, presenting the award for best song, opened the sealed envelope and surprised...had to announce himself as winner. 'I'm glad to present the award', he said. 'I've known the fellow for a long time'."

Classic favorites Gary Cooper and Jimmy Cagney.

. . . in attendance lovely Hedy Lamarr.

Winners in wartime Van Heflin, Greer Garson, Jimmy Cagney and Teresa Wright.

Greer Garson's acceptance speech, when receiving the Oscar from Joan Fontaine for "Mrs. Miniver" was the longest in Academy history. For nearly an hour, she winged on thanking everyone who had ever helped her in her career. The cause for many jokes and a following rule that in the future all speeches would be limited to 3 minutes, Garson remained good natured about it. Several years later while taking part in an Oscar ceremony, she told the audience "If we have time, I have a few things left over to say..."

Robert Osborne, recognized authority and historian of the Academy Awards reported of this presentation, the last of the intimate banquets, "Some industry-ites still sadly shake their heads today and say, 'since they stopped having those banquets, the awards haven't been the same. They lost the festive spirit and gaiety of those early dinners and took on the larger dimensions that have continued to grow through the years.' "

And grow Oscar has continued to do beyond even the wildest press agent calculations. The little gold statue has become powerful enough to send a complacent career into orbit or help add several million dollars to a business investment. And his audience has grown from the original 200 to an international audience of 300,000,000 spectators in 60 countries!

Greer Garson in a marathon "thank you" and presenter Joan Fontaine.

Joan Bennett and Walter Wanger.

Producers Mervyn LeRoy and Darryl Zanuck bracketing Spencer Tracy.

On the occasion of Oscar's last intimate affair at the Ambassador, President Roosevelt's message was, "In total war, motion pictures, like all the human endeavor, have an important part to play in the struggle for freedom and survival of democracy. Those who achieve highly in motion pictures at this time have contributed greatly toward this end."

Ann Margret and "The Duke."

# And the Winner Is...

"Oscar" had moved, but Jennifer Jones, Ingrid Bergman, Ray Milland, Rosalind Russell, Gregory Peck, Jane Wyman, Olivia De Havilland, Fred Astaire, Gary Cooper, Susan Hayward, Audrey Hepburn, Spencer Tracy, Carol Channing, Anne Bancroft, Dustin Hoffman, Mike Nichols, Marilyn Monroe, Robert Taylor, Grace Kelly, Marlon Brando, Judy Garland, Kim Novak, Shirley MacLaine, Kirk Douglas, James Dean, Elizabeth Taylor, Frank Sinatra, Doris Day, Zsa Zsa Gabor, Bob Hope, Danny Kaye, Glenn Ford, Warren Beatty, Paul Newman, Sidney Poitier, Omar Shariff, Bing Crosby...and many, many others came back to pick up awards in the Cocoanut Grove. Their Golden Globe Awards.

Running a close second to the Oscars, the Golden Globes were originated by and for the foreign market...which accounts for considerable of Hollywood film distribution. Made up of the correspondents who belong to the Hollywood Foreign Press Association, it was inaugurated in 1944.

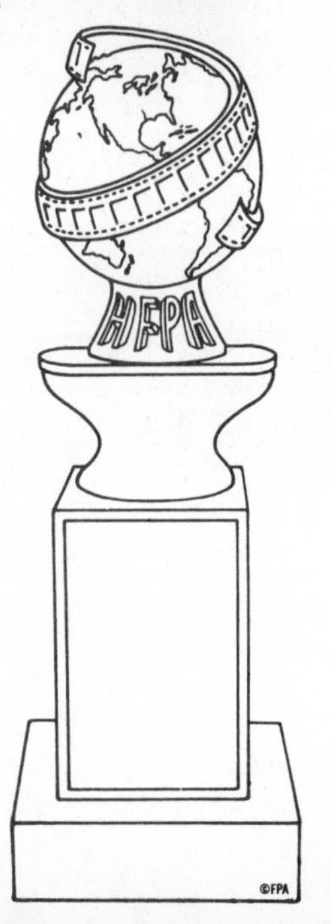

**LUCKY TABLE**—Mr. and Mrs. John Wayne and Mr. and Mrs. Hal Wallis occupy a winning table at the Golden Globe Award festivities. The actor and the producer received a total of five Golden Globe awards.

Henry Gibson, Carol Burnett and Julie Sommers.

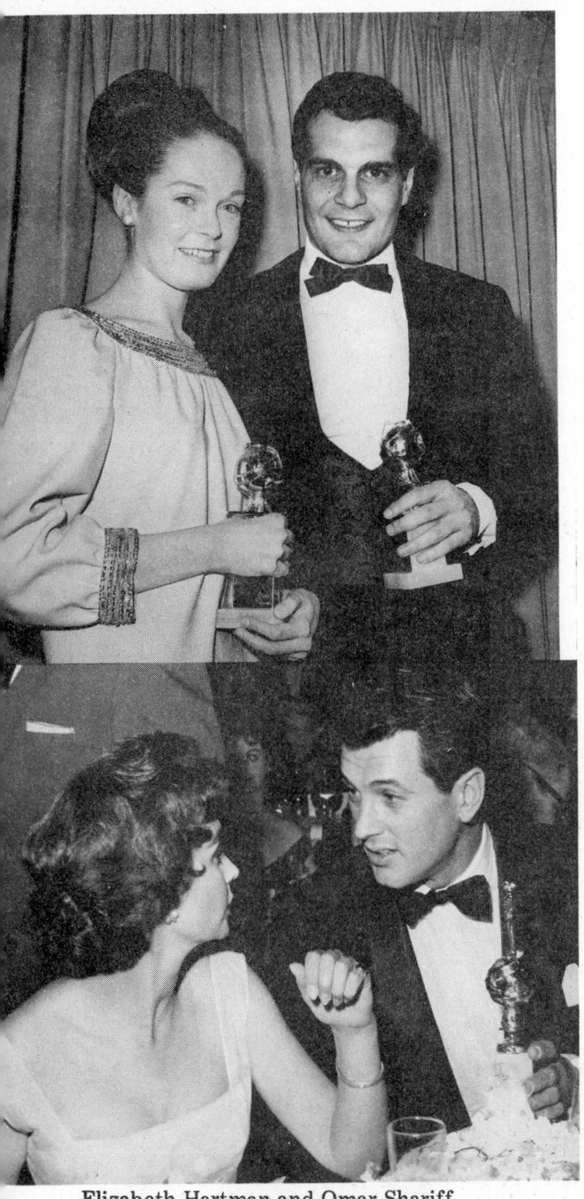

**Elizabeth Hartman and Omar Shariff.**
**Jean Simmons and Rock Hudson.**

**Handsome Lloyd Haynes from ROOM 222 and Patty Duke.**

Some of the members are as exotic and colorful as the stars they cover. Conspicious and fascinating among them are the Unger twins, Bertil and Gustav, a natty, mustachioed duo who correspond for Scandinavian publications. They both wear monocles, and are distinguishible only because Bertil wears his in the left eye and Gustav in the right...

At the 1954 Awards banquet, the Unger twins got into a fuss with another set of twins, Aly and Amad Sadick, cotton brokers and importers. Fists began flying and it was impossible for the audience to tell who was doing what to whom. However, when hotel attendents broke it up, there were black as well as monocled eyes in evidence. In an event noted for dramatic and apprehensive moments, this episode was clearly the winner. And reported to the whole world...by the foreign press.

In its early days, the organization was not considered very authentic, rather it was open-handed both in deciding winners and in disclosing their names before the event. Today, however, it has become vital in the industry; professional and something of a harbinger of winners prior to the Oscar presentations.

The Cocoanut Grove is ideal for award presentations, but lending even more reason to the Golden Globe use, was one of its early founders, Yani Begakis...long on the staff of the Ambassador.

Memorable was the Awards night when Hollywood's sex symbols Marilyn Monroe who won for SOME LIKE IT HOT...looking about as hot as they come, was upstaged by Vicki Dugan who arrived in a dress down to there, how shall I describe it...her back could be scratched clear down to her fanny.

And when 1979's Best Motion Picture Actress Sally Field accepted her award for NORMA RAE, she remarked she felt higher than the night as a presenter, and costumed as THE FLYING NUN, she flew across the ceiling of the Grove to land in the arms of a waiting on-stage John Wayne.

# More Winners

Contending and "awards" may have been born with the Oscars...and since the first of them was presented in the Cocoanut Grove, literally thousands of them have been bestowed on anxious and most times deserving recipients in the room as well as in other banquet halls in the hotel.

Most memorable have been the Foreign Press "Golden Globes"...in some years almost as coveted as Oscars. Emmy's, Golden Records, Los Angeles Drama Critics, Academy of Science and Fiction, loving cups for Miss California Universe, Miss Black America, Miss Tiny Tot, Wampus Babies, Miss American Teen, Miss World, Photoplay Awards, Miss U.S., and not to be overlooked, the Queen of Female Impersonators. This latter award, every bit as glamorous as the Academy's.

(Clockwise): Ambassador Wally Smith and Miss Universe. Beauty comes in all packages in a California Beauty Pageant. More beauties . . . including the San Francisco Giant's baseball great Willy Mays. Miss Wilshire Chamber of Commerce. Little Beauties . . . waiting in the wings to grow up. Overgrown MB with Miss USA.

# International Beauty Queens

The very first (in the world) beauty contest held for senior ladies was a big sensation . . . with both the pretty ladies and their families, and particularly the press. Hundreds had to be turned away from the pageant which selected Sue Coleman as the winner and eight charming runner-ups(from age 60 to 92) including: Edna Williams 73, daughter of slaves, who does volunteer hospital work; ex-Ziegfield Follies girl Towyna Thomas; Eva Strange, whose husband once was a contender for the job of California Governor; 63 year old Sylvia Smith . . . looking 45; Lupe Sillas, mother of a high ranking government official; Etta Morrison, at 92 goes dancing twice a week; career woman Mildred Jefferds; Rosalee Harmon, once the wife of society band leader Manny Harmon; and winner school teacher Sue Coleman.

Clockwise from top: "Effervescent" Sylvia Smith; Sue Coleman with Mayor Sam Yorty; Towyna Thomas with her trophy; Berenice Janssen, also ex-Follies beauty, Hollywood actress and mother of actor David Janssen (and winner of subsequent SBC crown); Sue drying her tears of happiness on the Mayor's handkerchief with Lupe Sillas and Miss California Carol Marie Herrema looking on; Sue greeting her fans.

**Clockwise: Actor Burgess Meredith. Audience. Gayna Shireen "Miss Science Fiction" with Dick Benjamin and Paula Prentiss and George Burns at microphone. George with Charlton Heston. Darth Vader, pretty girls and Mark Hamill of STAR WARS (the evening's big winner).**

Darth Vader from Outer Space stalking the Cocoanut Grove? Another first. The humanoid was the presentor for the first televised awards program of the Academy of Science, Fiction and Horror films. KTLA televised the show for the organization founded by Dr. Donald Reed a few years previous. It has an enormous membership and is one of the fastest growing groups in the country...such is the heavy interest in these themes.

By GREGG H

The theater is much a man's wo to the Los Ang Critics Circle wh presented 22 re and 13 special to male recipien evening at the Hotel.

A celebrity l 200, representi of show busines a festive cock banquet in the Room to hon of the sou organization's poll.

Early las Angeles' fa dor Hotel v the third an of the Adul ion of Am roducers, eater ow m busi ntry sh o-day s s e s eview

WINNERS—Connie Chung and Jess Marlow picked up awards at Los Angeles Area Emmys.
Times photo by Bob Chamberlin

## Loring, Buttram Emmy entertainer:

Gloria Loring and Pat Buttram wi entertain at the Academy of Tel Area Emm

## Photoplay Awards set for Sept. 23, airs later on ABC

Annual Photoplay Gold set as a 90- TV for No- vin T. Vane, m director, movie and based on na- ed by Photo- Previous reci

## Cronkite to Speak at Awards Banquet

Walter Cronkite, managing editor of "CBS Evening News," will be guest speaker at the fourth an sional Awards Banquet of Los Angeles chapt ciety of Professional Journalists, Sigma Delta the Embassy Room of the Ambassador Hotel.

Presentation of 1979 awards will be made to ter Stan Chambers of KTLA and city hall re Peterson of the Valley News. The awards re nificant achievement and/or consistent perf professional journalist presenting the news perspective, accuracy and fairness."

## Cronkite to at Awards Ba

Walter Cronkite, managing edito News," will be guest speaker at the sional Awards Banquet of Los Angeles chapter of the So- ciety of Professional Journalists, Sigma Delta Chi, Dec. 1 in the Embassy Room of the Ambassador Hotel.

## KTLA, KNXT Share Emmys

BY JAMES BROWN
Times Staff Writer

KTLA's landmark documentary, "Scared Straight!" and KNXT Channel 2 shared honors at the 31st annual Los Angeles Area Emmy Awards, presented Sunday night at the Cocoanut Grove.

## Critics give awards

Clockwise: Founder Dr. Donald Reed with Gary Kurtz, producer of STAR WARS and actor William Shatner. Shatner with Karen Black. Hamill with Olympic Swim Champion Buster Crabbe and portrayer of DRACULA, Christopher Lee.

Tawny Tann

BRANDY LEE
*"Miss Cotillion – 1972"*

Mr. Ronnie Summers

## More Awards
## Girls or Boys?

One former queen, a beautiful, sultry, supple-limbed *man*...dramatically entered the Grove down the grand staircase to the strains of "A PRETTY GIRL" dressed in shimmering white satin. Breast, derriere and all component parts undulated as provocatively as under any white satin that ever adorned a Jean Harlow or Marilyn Monroe. Wearing what could have been the equivalent of a million dollars worth of jewels, and leading two pure white, elegant Russian Wolfhounds he was a vision of...loveliness?

The entertainment was part of the contest, and for the most part, terrific as performed by dozens of male impersonators who competed. Half the audience was straight-looking men, young and old, dressed in ivy league or evening attire, who were escorting other men in exquisite female clothing, jewels, furs and high heels which sent some of them up to heights several inches above their escorts.

One of the few females present, I was fascinated and stayed through the very last act. (Never could figure out which rest room to use.)

As ambitious as the evening began however, the boys didn't have the staying power girls have achieved in the restrictions of high fashion. By midnight, wigs were askew, dangling earrings were pulled off and in beaded purses, meticulously manicured nails were being chewed. Flower corsages were as wilted as the long legs and high-heeled feet whose long skirts and trains were pulled up over knees, which were spread apart man-fashion and worn out.

In the immortal words of Joe E. Brown spoken to an in-drag Jack Lemmon in SOME LIKE IT HOT, "Nobody's perfect."

## "Home Away From Home"

The Ambassador has been home to many thousands who have never spent a night under her roof.

The hotel's vast army of personnel has included innumerable people, often several members of one family; some clocking decades with the establishment; several since opening day; to whom it has provided a way of life and opportunities.

But in the beginning, assembling a staff for a new enterprise was difficult, recalled waitress Vera Walker. "California didn't yet have very many people trained in elegant service, so they had to be transported. (A special trans-continental train was chartered to bring in 100 employees who had been enticed from the East's finest inns). "We lived in town, and even the streetcars didn't come out this far to the 'sticks', so we had to walk the last 7 blocks."

Some of the early-day employees are still around. I have only to look out of my office window to the glorious gardens to see the life of one dedicated employee unfolded before me.

Frisco Mari, born of Italian parents in South America, was on the hotel's first garden crew, soon rising to and remaining in charge of the grounds. First employed by the Cotton family (one of the early owners) he was soon to become a force in the city as a designer of golf courses; one being El Rancho, at that time owned by the hotel for the pleasure of the guests who were chauffeured back and forth to it.

Next, Frisco supervised the building of the Cotton Ranch in San Clemente...later to be President Nixon's Western White House and home. From Washington the President personally wrote to Mari, praising the house and grounds.

Mari's young daughters were frequent visitors to the hotel, usually conscripted to "ride ponies and play with the little kids, children of royalty when they came to stay at the hotel."

Ursula Vils in writing about Frisco in the *Los Angeles Times,* said "The good things nearest his heart are the Ambassador grounds, the magnificent gardens that set it apart from any other metropolitan hotel.

"The hotel's fortunes are the story of America's life: Opulence in the 20's, receivership in 1930, mecca for the untaxed rich and great of the 30's, wartime's scarce labor and servicemen's parties in the 40's, financial gymnastics of Conrad Hilton and J. Myer Schine in the 50's, tragedy of Senator Robert Kennedy's assassination in the 60's." And through it all the gardens have remained a beautiful undisturbed oasis.

Mari planted banana, orange and lemon trees so that guests could pick their own fruit, and raised flowers so that they could be fresh in guest rooms every day. His staff numbered 25, and they tended 60,000 different varieties of shrubs and plants, and used almost 200,000 blooming plants a year.

Winter residents upon returning east were presented at the railroad station with a basket of Frisco's prize blossoms to take home.

Mari fondly recalls working with Abe and Ben Frank, father/son managers of the hotel in the 20's and 30's. "They treated me like family. The hotel gave me security and enabled me to raise a family and send my children to college." Reluctantly retiring only after serious surgery, to his horse ranch in 1976, he turned the reins of Groundskeeper over to his trusted assistant, Manuel Duarte.

But Mari held the reins on a second career which had been a result of his hotel association. "Mr. Cotton gave me a horse whose bloodlines are still in my stock inspiring the whole family to raise horses." Now the stock is part of a picturesque ranch Mari owns and operates with the help of his daughters. They are noted for the fine line of championship Arabians they show and breed...with some selling for as much as $100,000!

**Los Angeles Times columnist Jack Smith, Councilman John Ferraro congratulating Frisco Mari and his almost six decades of maintaining beautiful Ambassador guardens.**

Kosti Begakis who had starred in films in his native country of Greece brought his young family to America. "California, because it was similar to my own countryside, and because my brother Yani was here working at the Ambassador."

Kosti is still working at the hotel, as are his sons Mike and Nico. Working part-time while putting themselves through college, Mike is now a college professor, and Nico an accountant, and they still are associated with the hotel operating the expanded and modernized parking facilities.

Ambassador's Mike Begakis attending a Billie Jean King (tennis champ) and Assembly Speaker Robert Moretti press conference.

Two Mitsopulos brothers, coming to the hotel shortly after it opened, still will help out occasionally for elegant hotel parties. They recall serving President and Mrs. Roosevelt, sexy Jane Mansfield, Kate Smith, Elizabeth Taylor, Marlene Dietrich and Babe Ruth as highlights of their experiences, and in 1927, Colonel Charles Lindbergh, who, daily, would order only lamb chops, baked potato and strawberries. Tired of the dozens of sandwiches which were his only fare on his New York to Paris flight, no doubt.

Nick recalls Bing Crosby popping down several petit fours and not realizing "until they hit bottom that his buddies had sprinkled them with hot tabasco. Crosby didn't 'croon' that night!" he said.

He remembers well his own biggest blunder. King Paul of Greece was an honored guest, and the entire hotel was caught up in a flurry of security with uniformed officers all over the place. The morning after the arrival of the coterie, Nick carried breakfast to the king's suite. "The door was opened by a man in plain clothes and shirt sleeves. I laid the table, then, concerned that the food might cool, asked, 'Where the hell is the King' To which the gentleman, in a soft voice answered, 'I'm the King.' "

And what serves as protocol as in the royal problem that faced coffee shop hostess, Rose O'Donnell when the Sultan of Jabore fell in love with her...coming down to where she worked, dressed in his best formal evening attire...and every time she looked at him he would warmly smile his broad diamond capped tooth affection.

Paul Shahan, after 50 years of service, still enjoys coming back ("to get out of the house" he says) occasionally and work parties in the Grove. Looking and feeling amazingly fit, he says he is grateful to Maitre'd Tino Mendez for letting him work, and for giving him tables "close to the kitchen."

Previous room service manager Henry Carrillo, when first on the job had a call for a "Screwdriver" and "Wallbanger". He immediately dispatched representatives from maintenance and housekeeping.

Present room service manager Pepe Bautista's most vivid recollection is of the Robert Kennedy assassination, which was committed very close to his department and to which he was witness, helping to restrain killer Sirhan Sirhan.

☆ ☆ ☆

Bartender Jimmy Rychly said that "all of the employees were required to wear white gloves when royalty was in the hotel. Khrushchev liked the large display of vodka in the drug store when he arrived... but the Mrs. returned the bar and liquor that was set up for them in their suite. Not so with the press and his staff... so he visited them often.

"My most exciting moment was working the reception that was given for President Harry Truman. And the next time I saw him, you know, he remembered me? I was thrilled."

"Get that girl out of here!" said an outraged guest to the manager about an employee in one of the daily disasters that are not unusual in hotel life. But this particular circumstance had a happy ending.

A wealthy couple who had made even more money in the grain market in WWI, annually wintered in the hotel's most expensive and opulent suite. Pleased to see them in the lobby one morning, Juel, the cashier behind the cage, greeted them with "How are my Darlings this morning?" Mrs. Wife was furious, insisting that she had addressed Mr. Husband singularly...suggesting that something was going on that would cause Juel to call him her "darling" and demanding that she be fired. Subsequently Juel was dismissed, but only when the drug store manager agreed to hire her.

Mrs. Wife still was not satisfied and ultimately Juel left the hotel, and went off to work in Beverly Hills.

The happy ending? Juel established the most exclusive lingerie shop in the west, custom designing exorbitantly expensive negligees and intimate apparel for movie stars and wealthy clients...and without realizing who she was, for many years Mrs. Wife was one of JUEL PARK's steadiest clients...and guess who financed the shop!

Doorman Art Nyhagen has greeted hotel guests for almost 40 years.

35 year veteran Art Nyhagen remembers when the job of doorman was so lucrative and coveted that doormen paid for them. John Casey, who preceded him, became a wealthy man because of large tips and generous gifts of stocks. One appreciative guest treated him to a trip to his homeland, Ireland.

Art explains, "I like open air and exercise...and I like to greet people. How else would I get to meet John Foster Dulles, Nikita Khrushchev, the Crown Prince of Japan, the Crown Prince of Sweden...Peggy Lee and Dorothy Shay. When the Shah of Iran was here, his security men and our police were in attendance all the time. But he would get in his little sports car and elude all of them.

"Queen Juliana of the Netherlands asked to attend the Grove...and requested Liberace and Bob Hope to perform for her.

Howard Hughes used to park his beat up old car in the first stall so that he wouldn't be noticed when he slipped into it. And Mickey Cohen was a regular...friendly and a good tipper. Whenever he or his gangster buddies would appear on a headline in the newspaper, he would buy ten copies."

One of the hotel's very handsome doormen (doormen are always handsome) during the early twenties was famous according to Life Magazine, because of resident and writer Elinor Glyn's statement that in addition to red-headed sex-symbol Clara Bow, the only others in Hollywood to possess "IT" were Antonio Moreno, Rex, the Wonder Horse, and the doorman at the Ambassador!

Vera Walker enjoyed a particularly warm and close relationship with FBI Chief J. Edgar Hoover who spent his winter vacations at the hotel. Evidently the favorite of others as well, Vera inherited considerable money from one of her customers, jewelry and a diamond brooch from others. She retired in style.

And speaking of retiring...bellmen customarily check guests in...but not by choice "in" to bed. Endless are the bellmen tales...when they'll tell them. Some situations even embarrass *them* too much. It seems when some people are in towns where they are on "holiday", unobserved by family, friends or business associates, defenses and inhibitions quickly diminish.

Services Captain Kevin Veedana tells the story of a call he answered when an elderly gentleman offered him $10 to carry his young companion, too inebriated to make it on her own (his age precluded his doing the honors) into the bedroom and place her on his bed. When the gentleman asked Kevin to undress her, too, he declined...leaving without a tip.

But the one that puzzled Kevin, a tall, handsome and pleasant fellow, the most, was a call he answered to "Come get my bags," only to knock, and in answer to, "Come in," found the lady stretched out on the bed, totally nude. Answering her order to pick up her packed bags and take them to the cab stand preparatory to her departure, he checked all around the room, as is the bellmens' custom, and left. Nowhere in sight were any clothes. How she ever got out of the room and down to her cab...still bewilders him.

A bellman, by the very nature of his job, must be strong, pleasant, affable, and willing to serve his guests. Attendant to his job are the weird requests he gets...some proper, many illegitimate and improper.

Although hotels set policies, he is much on his own, and must decide for himself just what conduct will be his, and just how far he will go. A great deal of the reputation of the hotel rests with him. Liquor, during prohibition or after hours; marijuana; prostitutes; gays and who knows what-all are services frequently requested. Hardly a bellman exists who hasn't been propositioned himself, by both men and women.

A more mature Bell Captain revealed that when he was in his teens, a big problem was avoiding older men who would be willing to pay anything for "personal" favors and attention.

On one occasion, an attractive young lady was escorted to a single room (lower room rate than a double). She was observed entering the bar, "picking up" males and leaving with them, with more than logical or possible physical frequency. Security was alerted...the comings and goings were mystifying...leaving no in-between time for dressing, freshening up, etc. The security officer thought he was seeing double. He was...identical twin sisters, taking "turns"!

Somehow hotel work and life has a charisma, a friendliness, a sense of belonging that brings people back time and again. Former coffee shop manager Todd Jones, after decades of service, and retirement, still comes in to help out during peak times. Todd recalls, "We had all the Hollywood crowd here. Sid Grauman was a resident, and after all of his premieres at the Chinese Theatre, he and his friends would come in for coffee and conversation. Chaplin, all 3 Barrymores and Edward G. Robinson all lived here in bungalows at the same time. Like any ordinary neighbors, they would drop in to borrow glasses, silver and so on for their parties, then I would have to go round them up."

Jim Rychly and Carl Ezell with (center) Cesar Sandoval, winner of 1980 U.S. Bartender Guild Championship.

Maitre'd Tino Mendez celebrating film star Shaun Cassidy's 21st birthday in the hotel.

(Clockwise): Resident Manager Edward Ingle. Resident Adela Rogers St. Johns congratulating General Manager Fred Gee upon the hotel's 4-star achievement. L'Escoffier Award Winning Chef Marvin Slaughter with Food and Beverage Manager Carl Ezell and Bartender Jimmy Rychly. Services Manager Kevin Veedana with bellmen platoon.

# A City Within A City

The lady seemed so mysterious and so private. And so alone. She lived in her suite for 20 years...alone, and went about her daily business, disturbing no one, not welcoming any advances, and never leaving the hotel grounds. Stories and conjectures about her ran the gamut for suffering an ill-fated love affair, to harboring a fortune in stolen money, to being the silent, back-street lover of a famous official. Or movie idol? Or politician? She was secretly amused with the enigma she knew she presented, but the explanation was really quite simple.

There are some hostelries wherein one can reside with all of their needs and desires accomodated, without ever leaving the lot. The Ambassador is one such. It is a city within a city, with not only housing, prepared meals, exercise, entertainment and sundries supplied, but services as well. Thus, the permanents and regulars of the hotel have the world brought to them. Add to that the glamour of prominent and film people around a good deal of the time, making appearances, meeting with others, etc., in fact, supplying a social life.

No mystery, as the guest explained to me. "I would be so lonely anywhere else. But here there is always something going on. It fills my life".

If there was an "official" catalyst at the Ambassador that brought together film people, society, the rich and famous, it was *Robert Anstead.* A third generation jeweler, Bob catered to them all in his exclusive jewelry store in the hotel. Recognized as one of the most celebrated connoisseurs of fine antique silver, crystal and porcelain, he introduced gracious dining to ladies of Los Angeles, later advising their daughters in bridal gifts and etiquette. It was he who imported the first Beef Tables with their Sheffield covered venison dishes and services from England. He invented a silver utensil for grating cheese at the table. But the pepper grinder he brought back from London and introduced to California was the most popular of all. He presented a 30-inch mahogany mill to Alex Perino to use in his fine restaurant. That very same night a diner ordered 50 of them at $100 apiece.

Gold plated phones which he designed became popular with the film set. Marie Dressler bought several for her friends. A few days before Christmas, Anstead's was a scene of excitement and glamour, according to Lucy Toberman in SOCIETY WEST. Not only did the town's socialites flock to the Ambassador on a last minute shopping spree, but the theatre's greats as well.

Norma Shearer, Maurice Chevalier, Cecil B. DeMille, Constance and Norma Talmadge, Jack Dempsey, Estelle Taylor, Charles Chaplin and William Randolph Hearst were "steadies." Customers could depend on Anstead's suggested gifts because he usually knew the recipient and what gifts had already been purchased for that person.

Bob was known to keep the secrets of his clientele, for oftimes purchases were made that required discretion. But one story can now be told.

It was during a period when the entire Hearst family frequently used the hotel. The guest register indicates that at times William R. Senior would be in residence with his companion Marion Davies...on other occasions, the Hearst sons would be registered, sometimes with their mother or other chaperones. Seemingly considerate of one another, no disturbing conflicts were ever evident.

"One afternoon an elegant lady came into the store shopping for a birthday gift for a gentleman," explained Bob. I showed her several items, then suggested that if I knew who the gift was for I could better help her. I usually knew whose birthday was being shopped for, and what gifts had already been designated for that person. She avoided saying who it was for, but said that this gentleman particularly liked old clocks and unique picture frames. I showed her some clocks, then remembered some frames that had just arrived, and had not yet been unpacked. They were exquisite and expensive, of finely etched silver. I called to one of the girls to bring one out. As in the manner of frames, this one had a photo of a girl in it. A movie star, no less...Marion Davies.

"The customer smiled, said she liked it and told me to gift wrap it. She would take it with her. As this was being done, I wrote out the order and asked her if she wished to charge it. 'Yes, just charge my room number 517. My name? *Mrs.* William Randolph Hearst!' After I recovered from the shock...I realized that the lady had a great sense of humor."

Nikita Khrushchev's stay at the Ambassador was memorable for Anstead. "The Premier" did a double take when he passed by the store accompanied by a vast welcoming committee...then came back later when he escaped from his many bodyguards. I snapped a photo of him smiling as he viewed the rare collection of icons and Russian Imperial treasures in our display window. One oriental pearl icon was from the palace of Catherine the Great, a malachite mantel set and a set of silverware from the Leningrad Palace of Prince Youssoupf who was noted for extinguishing Rasputin."

Mr. and Mrs. *Robert Martin* bought the jewelry store from Anstead in 1960 and even without the Rasputins, Khrushchevs and Hearsts, have continued to provide the same fine quality to customers who return year after year (frequently attending annual seminars and taking gifts back to stay-at-home wives). Graduate Gemologist Martin displays sparkling, exquisite gems and solid gold masterpieces in his windows. Hard to resist. The shop, furnished in Oriental carpets and antique chairs with cushions needlepointed by Mrs. Martin is a gem itself.

The doyenne of the Ambassador...of Los Angeles' art world as well...is a petite, raven-haired aristocratic little lady who presides over the *Dalzell-Hatfield Gallery*. Ruth Hatfield's late husband Dalzell was deep into the arts with another gallery when it opened in the hotel; a few years later to establish his own which is recognized as the most authoritative in the city today.

Among the world famous art works they have handled are Rembrandt, Van Dyke, Gainsborough and Romney. Their gallery was the first in the West to specialize in modern French art such as Gauguin, Van Gogh, Cezanne, Renoir, Lautrec, Monet, Picasso, and other important masters...followed by the German Expressionist greats. Their faithful clients have followed the Hatfield advice, and watched their fine treasures appreciate beyond belief. The Hatfields aided many avid art lovers, helping to begin the collections of such as Norton Simon and Edward G. Robinson.

Notables at one of the many receptions of the Hatfield Ambassador Art Gallery showing the paintings of Cathleen Mann, Marchioness of Queensbury, were (standing) Louis Golding, famous author; Dalzell Hatfield, Mrs. Dalzell Hatfield; (seated) Cathleen Mann; Lady Hardwicke; Mrs. Edward G. Robinson.

**Another gallery reception attended by popular film star Charles Boyer (later to commit suicide because of depression caused by the loss of his beloved wife), actress Agnes Moorehead, Sir Cedric Hardwicke and Charles Laughton.**

**"Fantasy Island's" Mr. Roark, Ricardo Montalban with artist Mrs. Alfredo Ramos Martinez at showing of her famous husband's paintings.**

Many American artists have become famous through the gallery's exhibits, such as Sicard, Lutz, Gluckman, Cowles and Millard Sheets. Presently, in addition to fine oils and watercolors, the gallery specializes in fine antique and modern tapestries.

*Taffy's* has dressed film stars both personally and in films. Designing and manufacturing her own fashions, she at one time owned and operated a chain of 12 stores, selling them off to retain only the Ambassador shop. Recently retiring, she turned the store over to her very capable son, Richard Roberts. It seems to run in the family, as her daughter has just opened another Taffy's in Century City.

Liberace will buy all of the "pianos" she can get... jewelry ones, that is... from Henrietta Henry's *Jewel Box.* Featuring ladies suits and dresses, sweaters, millinery and boutique specialties, they usually wend their way to the shop after club and social luncheons.

Actor Robert Young, Mayor Sam Yorty, orchestra leader Fred Waring, and TV's "DALLAS" mean old "J.R." can frequently be seen shopping in the exclusive *London Shop,* for sophisticated and elegant men's wear.

Souvenirs, leather goods, stuffed toys, magazines, novelties, candy and overnight accessories are available in the *Something Special* Gift Shop... where foreign and out-of-state visitors like to browse.

Audio-visual and convention services are available from the *Photo & Sound Company*... necessary to all hotel functions.

California is at its colorful best in the *Ambassador Flower Shop* which greets guests at the front door. Operated by Margaret and Lawrence Pie, young transplants from Taipan have the Oriental artistic touch in creating beautiful arrangements.

*Penelope's Imported Gifts* is named for their Mother and operated by sisters Cathy Hogan and Marcy Harrison. They feature imported handcrafted items "bringing Europe to you" of vases and pottery, ethnic jewelry, plaques, embroidered pillows, fur rugs and other unique art.

Conveniently located *House of Scotland* features precious Cashmere sweaters for men and women, as well as stylish blouses and accessories.

*Dollar-A-Day* rents all makes of cars for seeing and cruising the wide environs of the city.

If you want to see more than drive, take one of the many *Gray Line Ambassatours* to see the Grand City; Beverly Hills and movie star's homes; Magic Mountain; Universal Studios; Disneyland; Knotts Berry Farm; Marineland; or if you feel adventurous, there's a Catalina Cruise or foreign and exotic Tijuana.

Or try *California Parlor Car Tours* which has operated quality motorcoach tours in California since 1924. Guests stay in the best hotels, see all there is to see and travel in comfortable coaches. They operate 3-Day and 4-Day Tours the year around from Los Angeles to San Francisco, visiting all the points of interest between the two cities as we travel along the beautiful Highway #1 via Big Sur. We visit Santa Barbara, the Danish community of Solvang, "Hearst Castle, Carmel, Monterey, 17 Mile Drive and terminate in San Francisco on the last day. Our 6-Day Tour includes beautiful Lake Tahoe and operates from May thru October."

*World Airline's* desk can transport you to dreamy Honolulu and other points east, west, south and north.

Tourism British Columbia's Ambassador Hotel office represents the *Government of British Columbia, Canada,* in Southern California. They assist travel industry representatives, media people, and individual travelers with information on Canada's west coast province in order to encourage travel to our area.

"The hotel has become a center for ticketing," so says *Ambassador International Travel* president Brian Clewer, whose bustling office combines tripping to everywhere with his *Continental Shop* which brings to you imports, phonograph records, beverages, art works, books, gifts, foreign newspapers and magazines from around the world. . . without leaving Wilshire Boulevard.

Clewer keeps everyone abreast of what is happening "over there" with his "British Radio Programmes" CYNIC'S CHOICE which is in its 20th year.

*Sadie Papazian, Electrolysist* has been located in the hotel for 37 years. She says, "I've seen a lot of changes . . . some bad, some good . . . but it's 'home' to me."

*Dentist Dr. Lloyd Robinson* began practicing in the hotel in 1938. How's that for endurance! His long-time patients are loyal . . . one Chicagoan flies to Los Angeles twice a year just for her teeth cleaning appointments with him!

*Norden Displays* are unique advertising and display specialists who handle hotel show-cases and the In-Lobby electronic console display. The console offers information on department stores, restaurants, and other services including: medical, limos, charter air, sightseeing, etc., and provides a direct telephone for additional information. In their office, John McLewee, Al Weissman and Jolie Mandell are "at your service," as well.

When Ambassador Health Club member Charles Berliner, a theatrical designer, became Western Regional Representative of his Union, *United Scenic Artists*, Local 829, he recognized that the Ambassador provided convenient accessability to the post office, restaurant, hotel and conference rooms suitable for the various business activities of the Union.

Founded in 1918 as an autonomous local of the Brotherhood of Painters and Allied Trades and affiliated with A.F.L.-C.I.O. United Scenic Artists has jurisdiction over certain creative arts and crafts for theatre, opera, ballet, motion picture, television, industrial show and exhibition industries. The Local is an association of artists and craftsmen, many of them world famous, organized to protect craft standards, working conditions and wages, and represents over 200 Scenery, Costume, and Lighting designers residing in the thirteen Western States. Colorful posters of famous theatrical productions designed by members of United Scenic Artists adorn their office walls.

**Margaret Burk and Marylin Hudson pose with Dorothy Shreve (chief instructor for the Burk/Hudson Beauty, Charm and Fashion Tour).**

The *U.S. Suburban Press* offices represent the most innovative idea existing today in newspaper advertising. It's a "one-stop" placement service through their representation of hundreds of suburban newspapers.

A *Rotary* office is maintained in the hotel for the Wilshire Club which has met in the hotel for 48 years.

Tennis is king in the *Tennis and Health Club* owned by *Starcrest Enterprise* and managed by proprietors, Abax and Mona Hamad. Ten lighted courts are provided for play and competition, with resident professionals conducting classes and clinics . . . or for practice, there's the automatic ball machines. The Health Club features sophisticated gym equipment, exercise classes, massages and Solana Tanning equipment, sauna, whirlpool, putting green, even a jogging track. For refreshers, there's the sparkling swimming pool and sun deck.

No gal can escape looking good if she avails herself of the complete beauty services of *Antonio's Cosmopolitan Salon.* Featuring the latest in fashion and techniques, Antonio also serves his profession. A member of the California State Board of Cosmetology for eight years, two as President, he was appointed under two governors. As a long time member of the Coiffure Guild of Los Angeles and Hollywood whose group annually held their beauty and trade shows at the Ambassador, Antonio worked with other dedicated members to make it a most prestigious show whose trophy to contestants was tantamount to a movie Oscar.

Nic Epright keeps the fellows looking good with haircuts, shaves and shampoos in the *Ambassador Barber Shop,* which also doubles as a meeting place for friends.

Last and not least is *Burk/Hudson Public Relations,* for which Burk would get killed by Hudson if it were omitted.

Barber shops are the usual domain and meeting place for a hotel male population . . . matter of fact, in querying around for information for this chapter, I, who consider myself somewhat knowledgeable in hotel lore was surprised to learn that often business is conducted therein with "ladies of the evening" or morning and afternoon for that matter. One popular hotel in downtown Los Angeles actually (unknown to management) had facilities in the barber shop back room for immediate (or emergency) service!

Manicurist Mary McNally

Of earlier days manicurist Mary McNally recalls "I have held more interesting hands than anyone in Hollywood, I guess," in the 20 years I was at the hotel, except for my girl-friend Anita Carney who stayed longer than I did. We did everything together in those days. Remembering, Mary tells about, "Sid Grauman used to come knocking on the door just at closing time after playing cards all day, so Nita and I would each take a hand to do his nails. He lived at the hotel and loved to gamble, but evidently wasn't very good. He lost all the time, even losing his furniture to Joe Schenck before he moved into the hotel.

"Gambling on one thing or another was a game with all of us. I remember betting the house physician that Notre Dame would beat S.C. in football...Notre Dame lost, so I had to give him manicures for a year. But when I had my appendix out, that sweet man sent me a bill marked 'paid in full'.

"We used to be 'on call' for manicures, and weren't supposed to go without a barber, but we got to know our customers so well that management didn't worry about us. When we went to the Talmadge for Joe Schenck, he would send us home in his limousine...but not until after we had a nice dinner in his apartment. Everybody seemed to have limousines and chauffeurs. Abe Lyman used to lend me his to take my Mother out on Sundays, but we had a real great time the summer we were loaned Mr. William Randolph Hearst's limo and chauffeur when he and Marion went to Europe. We went up to visit the Hearst Castle for the week-end, and spent much of our summer vacations driving around in real luxury.

"Mr. Boudet, who owned a buggy and auto tops company (later selling out to Fisher Bodies) enjoyed my greeting him by name each winter when he came back. He used to tip me $5 and $10 gold pieces. And when he left, he always put a hundred dollar bill in my hand.

"Howard Hughes was very young, and a favorite around the hotel. He never got manicures, but when he came in for a haircut, there was no tip, just a smile.

"We had many distinguished foreign patrons. Once a whole polo team came over from Spain, and another favorite of mine who owned stables and came to the Ambassador for the horse shows, was a Prince from Casablanca, Morocco.

"Once we were hired to appear in a movie, BATTLE OF THE SEXES that was filmed in the barber shop. Jean Hersholt was the star, and when we didn't finish until 5 in the morning, he was nice enough to drive me home. I remember it so well...he parked the car, and together we saw the sun rise over the ocean.

"One very wealthy drug store chain owner used to run over from E.F. Hutton across the hall where he was watching the stock market reports, jump into the chair for a shave. With his hat in one hand and his cigar in the other he would say, 'Once over lightly', and not even let the barber recline the chair. Always in a hurry, he explained, 'While I'm sitting here, I could lose a million dollars.' And on October 29, 1929, when the stock market crashed...he did!"

"I enjoyed my job and the people. Orchestra leader Sid Lippman autographed a photo for me, 'To Mary, who polishes my spirits as well as my hands.' "

Other renowned individuals figure in the behind-the-scenes hotel services and activity. Jacqueline Cochrane, famous for her daring "firsts" in the aeronautical world, both as a flyer and woman (she pioneered and headed the women's Ferry Command during WW2) once leased and operated the hotel beauty shop. When I contacted her, she was reluctant to talk about it. She had not been satisfied with her working relationship with the hotel, and evidently considered it an unimportant part of her life. She recommended to learn about her, that I read her biography which I did. Terrific...as she herself is...a dynamite lady. But no mention of the shop.

However, the Ambassador must have exerted some influence in her life as it was the early center of aeronautical pioneering in the state.

HIGH FLYERS
Famous meeting requested by astronaut Neil Armstrong with music-great Duke Ellington. Looking on, Linda Garcia and Harry Burk. In the hotel for a week-long seminar with the Peace Corps, Armstrong had reached a saturation point of meeting thousands of people all around the world as part of the duties of the first man who walked on the moon. As a courtesy we asked if there was any particular person left (!) that he would like to know in Los Angeles. Surprisingly there was. He would like to meet Duke Ellington (who was at that time appearing at the Grove). Duke was delighted . . . and at the meeting, in his typical fashion, bussed Armstrong on both cheeks. They reminisced about the moment when Armstrong took his first step on the moon. Ellington was playing a concert at Dartmouth University, Armstrong's alma mater. The song? An Ellington composition . . . "Moon Walk."

Russian Astronauts enjoying entertaiment at the Grove with American Astronaut Buzz Aldren and entertainer Anthony Newley.

Apollo X Astronauts Eugene Cernan, John Young and Thomas Stafford greeting the community on the lawn of the Ambassador with MB.

# "Balloons to Moons"

The chauffeur smoothly weaved the Mercedes Benz down the ribboned freeway through the skyscraper canyons of Los Angeles toward the openness of the road and the sandy mesquite rolling hills of the desert.

I was thoroughly enjoying this luxury...plus the day away from it all with Mr. Bob Anstead, owner of the hotel jewelry shop for 34 years until he sold to present proprietors, Mr. and Mrs. Robert Martin. Bob was thrilled to find that the hotel book was being written.

In Palm Desert, he introduced me to Mr. and Mrs. Cliff Henderson...she the beautiful film star Marian Marsh, and he the originator and early developer of that popular community (between Palm Springs and Indio) where Presidents Eisenhower and Ford, Bob Hope, Frank Sinatra, Phil Harris, Bing Crosby and other golfers and sun lovers build their winter homes.

Bob was eager for me to meet Henderson, as he not only is considered one of the pioneering aeronautical greats...but had headquartered in the hotel while pursuing these accomplishments. Henderson maintains a museum collection...a veritable history of aviation.

Credited with keeping aviation alive in the early days, when people were just becoming accustomed to the "horseless" carriages and slow to believe that motored vehicles could stay in the air, Henderson took on the impossible chore of conducting the National Air Races. Several were held in Los Angeles at the old Mines Field, at that time a 640 acre bean and barley field (presently International Airport) which Henderson later managed.

The Ambassador's Ben Frank, along with other forward thinking pals such as Jimmy Doolittle, Roscoe Turner and Amelia Earhart maintained a Flying Club in the hotel. Ben also supplied a suite for the National Air Races use in the hotel for months at a time in preparation for the races.

Notable for unprecedented excitement were the 1928 races. However, originally prospects were dismal as times were tough and many people were out of jobs. The races were underwritten by several oil companies, but still there wasn't much money, motivation or interest in such frivolity. Henderson wasn't anticipating much of a turnout. Opening day, the crowd was even more sparse than he anticipated, and a tragic accident didn't help the prospect of future days' attendance. Daring aces and Army and Navy teams competed in events which certified speed and altitude records, and when the sensational Army Air Corps acrobatic trio flew at too low an altitude, their leader crashed and was killed.

When a despondent Henderson returned to the hotel, a telephone call was waiting for him. "I picked up

Early air races and exhibitions in Los Angeles.

the phone to hear a familiar voice *ask* if he could please come down from Santa Barbara where he was visiting to take the place of the flyer who had crashed, for the remainder of the races. The offer was from a 25 year-old former farm boy who had become an airmail pilot and stunt flyer who had previously flown with the trio." Totally dedicated to the air, the daring young ace had electrified the world to become its hero of heroes by his unprecedented, 3,600 mile, epic solo flight from New York to Paris. It was the voice of Charles Lindbergh.

"I couldn't believe our good luck and his brave offer. But it did the trick. Our previously empty bleachers couldn't accomodate all of the people who came to see him. They closed their shops, schools and movie houses... and came by the thousands. Lindbergh flew every day...and we were a smashing success."

About Lindbergh...On the 50 year anniversary of the famous flight to Paris, the Herald Examiner wrote, "Today's young people cannot imagine how breathlessly an earlier generation awaited the result of his 33½ hour journey on May 20-21, 1927 battling snow, fog, rain and winds in his single engine plane, the Spirit of St. Louis. The experts said it couldn't be done. But he did it.

"The Lone Eagle's sensational flight fostered the age of air travel and air transport which since has zoomed us to the moon and Mars, bringing nations closer together, creating new industries, millions of jobs and billions in revenue."

The heroic Lone Eagle . . . Charles Lindbergh.

The Herald's publisher, William Randolph Hearst, then living at the Ambassador gave a magnificent ball for the flyer upon his arrival in Los Angeles. Even though "Lucky Lindy" could and did make heroic and monumental decisions in the air...the ballroom presented even more complex ones. This is the way the greatest story teller of our time, Adela Rogers St. Johns, saw it.

"Overnight this time truly overnight the Lone Eagle had become the greatest hero the United States has ever had. On his arrival in our film capital a short time after the ticker parade of the century in New York, Mr. Hearst entertained for Lindbergh at a beautiful *thé dansant* at the Ambassador. The guests included every star in the firmament plus all the brass in any field and their wives. Lindy, tall, slim, very quiet...looking back, I am sure he was still in a state of shock from all that had happened...sat at the head table between Mary Pickford and his hostess, Marion Davies. We were fond of *thé s dansants* in those days and it had many advantages over the later cocktail party in that soon everyone was *seated* at the flower-laden head table and all the smaller ones around the shining dance floor and Guy Lombardo's music began.

"A moment of silence prolonged into tension.

"If Lindbergh had ever drunk tea before it had undoubtedly been in a Harvey Eating House and he had no idea he was supposed to open the ball. We saw then that there was also involved a Social Predicament.

"If he takes Mary Pickford will this be adjudged an insult to Marion Davies? If he chooses Marion, will this violate protocol that nobody must step on the floor before an anointed queen? Moreover this is a clean young Galahad, idol of American youth, should he so honor the mistress, no matter how much we love her? Even if *we* didn't print it, everybody else would.

"Mr. Hearst needed no advice from his columnist Emily Post. With elephantine grace he moved. Before we could expel the breath we were holding he had offered his hand to Marie Dressler, conducted her regally to Lindbergh, and presented him to her. In less time than we got a new breath, the Grand Old Lady of the Movies, the incomparable unequaled and beloved Marie Dressler who was also friend and intimate of grand duchesses and society leaders, and Lindy had taken the floor together. We sat watching them. Gloria Swanson and I were reminiscing about this the other day as one of our shining memories. Recalling how we burst into applause and then cheers as the tall blond hero and the stately old lady moved the length of the floor and back alone in a waltz. Then Mr. Hearst indicated and Douglas Fairbanks, the Prince Consort, bowed to Marion and he himself took Mary Pickford out in royal fashion to join these couples who preceded him to the dance floor."

Later, Lindy confessed that to him, dance floor arenas were as dangerous as the big, blue sky he had conquered.

Aeronautical "first lady," Amelia Earhart.

"Why would anyone drop whatever else they were doing and rush to the Ambassador at the call of Amelia Earhart to volunteer to work for her? Because she was magnetic, sweet, charming and inviting," Captain Clarence Williams told the Zonta Club, a member of which Amelia was at the time of her death. "Amelia was a great woman. I still regard her as the glory of America."

She was planning her flight from Los Angeles to Newark, N.J. when she called him...and "a love affair began that is still going on", said Williams who worked with the famed aviatrix for several years, preparing charts for all of her flights. His accuracy put her only five miles off when she crossed the Ohio line on the Newark flight.

In answer to questions as to the loss of her plane and mystery of her disappearance on her subsequent flight around the world, he said, "I do not believe that she was captured by the Japanese. She was not on a spy mission, and there was no such equipment in her plane. Nor do I believe that Miss Earhart was imprisoned in the Imperial Palace in Japan from 1941 to 1945 as rumored...but it would have made a marvelous plot for a story."

One of Amelia's closest friends, Adela Rogers St. Johns doesn't agree. "I covered most of her flights...but this one was different. She was following some plan which she wouldn't speak of. I knew she had been in Washington before the flight, and when she told me goodbye, it was in such a way that I knew I would never see her again."

When I learned that Los Angeles was anticipating a visit from the Apollo X astronauts and their families, and that they would be helicoptered from a City Hall reception honoring them directly to another that was planned in Beverly Hills, then to a dinner at the Hollywood Palladium, I beseeched Governor Ronald Reagan and Mayor Sam Yorty to instead make them more available to turned-on and excited Angelenos between the two points. And so it was that Eugene Cernan, John Young and Thomas Stafford motorcaded the length of Wilshire Boulevard, each with their families in open cars to "land" on the lawn of the Ambassador, there on a hastily built grandstand to be greeted by Governor Ronald Reagan, Los Angeles Chamber of Commerce President John Vaughn, and Wilshire Chamber of Commerce President...me...along with officials from the hotel, and thousands of cheering fans.

Fresh from their lunar mission(!) the Governor told them that he was happy that they were seeing California from the ground! Their historic 577,000-mile space flight had included 31 lunar orbits and a scouting flight that had taken them 10 miles above the moon.

Modest young men, not nearly as impressed with their feat as were their admirers, we were reminded of the magnitude of their efforts by the newly built 35 story Equitable Building directly across the street. It is approximately the same height, 530 feet, as the launch structure which projected their spacecraft into orbit!

As guests of the Ambassador, the astronauts and their families enjoyed a restful sojourn "down to earth" in Los Angeles.

# "Playground for Kids, Too"

Young, happy and talented Deanna Durbin and Judy Garland.

How lucky for kids living in hotels with their parents. Imagine, tumbling out of your room and finding a Lindbergh or live Astronauts in your front yard. Those whose parents are hotel managers enjoy opportunities usually unaffordable and unavailable to most children. Especially in California where tennis courts and outdoor swimming pools are essential.

Add to it the playground, playhouse, archery range, roller rink, bowling alleys, nursery school, and their private dining room...even a peacock that flew over from McArthur Park to join the deer, birds, ducks, swans, and other animals in the hotel zoo. Shetland ponies were added when Queen Wilhelmina of the Netherlands arrived with her royal family. The young children were well-guarded and lonely until Frisco Mari brought over both the ponies and his daughters to keep them company.

Adult children also enjoyed zoo residents with which they played games on each other. Sid Grauman led one of the kangaroos over to Walter Winchell's bungalow as a gag...when the famous columnist arrived...all of the furniture had been knocked over by his hopping mad guest. Walter was pretty scared, staff remembers, and called for them to get the XX!#$ monster out of the place. And another time Joe "Ya wanna buy a duck?" Penner was obliged with a gaggle of his little feathered friends in his bathtub. John Barrymore on his "rounds", (favorite pastime: a glass of his bootleg booze in hand), would entreat the phone operators to baby sit his monkey Clementine when he worried she was lonely.

All of the guests attended the shower bearing fruits and vegetables on July 13, 1934 when twin fawns were born in the zoo. Walter Winchell acted as surrogate father and named the new babies. Earlier that same day, Bing and Dixie Crosby had become the father of twins Philip and Dennis...so two little four legged spindly spotted newcomers became their namesakes. Philip and Dennis Deer.

The demise of the zoo came to pass when a playful bear cub grew into a leg-chewing 100-pounder, and centered his voracity on the delicious if reluctant managing vice-president, Ben Frank. Wrong tid-bit...end of zoo.

Carlyn Frank Benjamin, grandaughter of manager Abe Frank and daughter of Ben who succeeded Abe, and her sister, were "hotel kids." Carlyn recalls, "We lived in the Rincon bungalow and Walter Winchell, his wife June and the children were a cottage away. The kids were our playmates as were other visitors and residents, children of stars and hotel personnel. My best friend was the son of the house detective."

The hotel was in receivership in the early thirties when Strauss and Cotton lost it. Even the slot machines in the Casino did little to alleviate financial problems...few people had loose change to play them.

Walking through the hotel grounds, Carlyn pointed, "We were sitting there in the dining room when the 1932 earthquake hit. Not much damage to the hotel...but frightening, especially to Easterners. Father set up a band in the lobby to calm everyone...and saved the day. That night everyone slept out on the lawns."

A telephone operator took a call from a guest who shouted, "I left a wake-up call, but this is riduculous!"

"Ben Bernie had a cabana poolside (a sandy beach had been imported...another 'illusion' for patrons) and would roll his piano out and entertain with his buddies Al Jolson, Eddy Cantor, resident Jimmy McHugh and others. I learned to swim from Fred Cady who coached the 1932 Olympic team right here...imagine...me and Buster Crabbe. I got up to 100 laps a day!

"Joan Crawford and Franchot Tone were romancing...but earlier Joan used to 'dance for her supper' in Charleston and Black Bottom contests." (Columnist Dorothy Manners was a good buddy of Crawford's...and remembers "in those lean years, the actress would return her winner's trophies to the hotel, the hotel would buy them back and subsequently she would win them again.)

"As young as we were, the Grove was the most exciting place in our world. We were allowed to watch Uncle Abe (Lyman) and other bands from the boxes or sound booth over the band stand...where KFI did Los Angeles' first remote broadcast from the Grove. I remember Eddie Duchin playing STORMY WEATHER with sound effects as the moving band stand worked over into the spotlight; Ozzie and Harriet; Veloz and Yolanda...Gower Champion who won Major Bowes'contest...and a young skinny kid from Hoboken, Frank Sinatra...who didn't." Not too many years later Sinatra was knocking them dead when he appeared at the Grove as a soloist with Tommy Dorsey and again, when *he* was the featured headliner.

Carlyn remembers a telegram from George Bernard Shaw in answer to a request to speak before a convention. In his cryptic way he said, "Thank you, but there is nothing I can think of that I would rather not do."

And then, of course, there were the drunken conventioneers and the camp-following prostitutes...and one harrowing episode of a participant laid out on the lawn, drenched in "blood" and apparently dead, until security wiped off the ketchup his companions had poured all over him.

Recalling her father's and his buddies practical jokes..."One evening, several of his friends were invited to meet a royal visitor, a duchess who, while seated on a long velvet couch regally offered her hand and invited the men to sit down beside her. Very beautiful and exotic, and with her foreign accent, she completely charmed them. A bit later, others came forward to meet her, and as she rose to greet them...her companions were startled to view the other side of the Duchess. The entire back of her dress was completely bare."

Walking through the East Garden, Carlyn seemed to be seeing an Easter Egg Hunt...traditional since the early days for crippled children...but then the big prize was a special egg... A real gold one from the Ambassador's fine jewelry store.

The winner! and Mrs. Sammy Davis.

While their parents were dining formally in the Fiesta dining room (now the Embassy) with its Chinese and Ballet Russe decor, listening to Mark Fisher's Chamber Music and peering through the walls of plate glass into the room's private gardens and romantic California nights, the children were not left to nursemaids or alone. They too had their private dining room. Built just for them, it was a continuing party. Decorated in happy colors and furniture to size, on the wall was painted this poem:

*I eat all my meals in Kiddie Land*
*Along with Little Jack Spratt,*
*And Polly Puts the kettle On...*
*Now what do you think of that.*

*And the Queen of Heart is Making Tarts,*
*While Jack Horner Pulls Out a Plum.*
*Oh, the Kiddie Land at the Ambassador*
*Is always so much fun.*

*For there's Miss Muffet on her Tuffet*
*And here's the Blackbird Pie...*
*And Simple Simon met with the Pie Man*
*And Peter Piper's wife in a Golden Pumpkin*
*Lives right near by.*

*With Mother Goose stories all around*
*Wouldn't you...in a room like that*
*Sing for YOUR supper*
*And laugh and eat with Little Jack Spratt.*

The Ambassador General Manager's son and daughter, Richard and Suzanne Gee.

**Early residents at a birthday party . . . Carlyn Frank Benjamin, second from left, and Paul Wallach in sailor suit.**

But there was one boy who didn't spend much time in Kiddie Land. From an early beginning, his was the appetite of an epicure.

Paul Wallach was one of the Ambassador's kids. Today his name is synonymous with elegance in the world of restauranteurs and diners. He is the author of an annual GUIDE TO THE RESTAURANTS OF SOUTHERN CALIFORNIA, and he hosts a popular restaurant talk show on Radio KIEV.

As a little boy Paul lived in the hotel with his society mother who was active as President of the Music and Art Foundation and his father. Paul tells how it all began for him:

"My love affair with restaurants began when I was six years old and my father became the house physician for the Ambassador Hotel in Los Angeles, and I found friends and happiness in the clattering, chattering, behind-the-scenes world of the busy kitchens, where I was immediately adopted by cooks and dishwashers and pantrymen and meat-cutters. After a while, I was allowed to set the tables in the banquet rooms. Stir the stockpots and taste the bearnaise and bordelaise sauces. The huge baker, his florid face dusted with flour, baked special cookies for me. The majestic chef would carry me on his shoulders during his inspection tour of the cooking area, rumbling things to me like "What you think, little pigeon, is that souffle" (or ice carving or salad dressing or duckling) "*ready* for our people?"

My best friend was a Filipino apprentice, scarcely bigger than I and a superb mimic. We used to sneak into the private rooms favored by wine and food societies, and as the distinguished-looking guests would raise their glasses, my friend would ape each expression—the quivering nostrils, the closed rapt eyes, the pursing of lips, the sage nods of approval—so perfectly that I was reduced to uncontrollable giggling and had to be dragged away to escape detection.

"On those occasions when I joined my family for dinner in the main salon, my friends would pretend except in little undetectable ways—not to know me. The maitre'd pinched me *hard* on the rear when I came in, and both of us maintained a straight face. Nor did I crack up when the filling in my baked potato turned out to be neither butter nor sour cream but *bavarois au marasquin* (my favorite cream dessert) nor when my souffle Grand Marnier had a grotesque cross-eyed face embroidered with dragees (sugar-coated bits of fruit). These eccentric, wonderful people were my friends, and I loved them."

Paul's father was an integral part of the hotel family as house physician to guests who lived there permanently, or for the long winter months.

# What's Up, Doc?

The stories a hotel house physician experiences are probably the hardest to come by, due to their built-in confidentiality. But one very prominent patient of Paul Wallach's father's was a legend and "character" not easily kept out of the public eye.

Wilson Mizner arrived at the Ambassador in 1927, there to spend the rest of his days. He pulled up at the wheel of his huge and ancient Packard...a remnant of the high times, wealth, and luxury along with adversity, abolishment, and discredit he had alternatingly experienced in his adventures among the rich and famous... vis-a-vis the underworld figures passing through his life.

Considered the "wit" of the century, vivid, wry, colorful and debonair, he was a talented playwright, albeit a talented bunco artist as well. He immediately enraptured the Hollywood community.

Mizner himself and his exploits was the characterization which Anita Loos, author of GENTLEMEN PREFER BLONDES later fashioned Clark Gable's role about the Barbary Coast in SAN FRANCISCO. Miss Loos worshipped the Mizner legend and was fascinated by his insouciance, and his slightly sinister reputation. Conversely, he was brilliant, witty and amusing. Miss Loos would frequently be among his circle of admirers and patrons listening to his rapier-like comments, and his charming and real-life adventures.

Famous wit Wilson Mizner.

Mizner's table in the Ambassador dining salon became a sparkling locale much like the renowned literary Round Table of the New York Algonquin for the group of so-called Well Known Authors who were at that time being hired by studios to upgrade the level of stories for films which were becoming sophisticated. Mizner subsequently was hired by Warner's as a writer...doing very little writing, but contributing greatly as a story doctor and creating plots that were incorporated into the burgeoning new style of gambling and underworld films.

Never one to be unobservant about a potential opportunity Mizner soon entreated his friend Herbert K. Somborn (recently divorced by Gloria Swanson when she married the Marquis de la Falaise de Coudray) who owned a piece of property on Wilshire opposite the Ambassador to build a restaurant. They inveigled producer Jack Warner into providing the financing, and the first of the Brown Derby restaurants, named by Wilson in honor of the headgear worn by two men he admired, Bat Masterson and Alfred E. Smith, was born.

Transferring his impeccably dressed person every night to the Derby, he routinely would confer with Bob Cobb (the manager of the Derby, later to become owner) then, he would hold court in Booth 50 which was always reserved for his coterie. Gossip columnists could always find material for their columns with the likes of Doug Fairbanks, Darryl Zanuck, Charlie Chaplin, Georgie Jessel, a maharaja...and Mae Murray and whichever Prince Mdivani she was married to at the time.

(Some years later, this same booth was occupied by Clark Gable and his wife Carole Lombard on the evening and prior to the Academy Awarding at the Cocoanut Grove when "GONE WITH THE WIND" and Vivian Leigh were winners to Gable's losing).

John Burke in his ROGUE'S PROGRESS said of the sage that he was a caustic commentator on show business with a lofty disdain for its less capable entrepreneurs. He became a leading figure in Hollywood during its transition period...and "instead of flattery, which he believed was the function of Louella Parsons and the fan magazines, he laid down a nightly barrage of insults, character assassinations and imprecations. It soon became an honor, of sorts, to have been insulted by Wilson Mizner.

"Mizner's scorn for the film industry was genuine, however," continued Burke, "and stemmed not only from a natural perversity but also from his nay-saying attitude toward most of the great events and hallowed personalities he had studied at close range. Born irreverrent, he refused to be impressed by anyone's pretentions; it was his chosen role to be a mocker and idol

**The famous original Brown Derby built by Wilson Mizner, Jack Warner and Herbert Somborn. At this writing the building is being demolished, and a new home is being sought for the "hat." The property is still owned by Gloria Daly, the daughter of Somborn and Gloria Swanson.**

smasher. He wasn't merely adopting an intellectual pose when he said, 'I don't know anything at all about this town. To me Doug (Fairbanks) and Mary (Pickford) are just a mule team. But after seeing some of the new pictures, I'm convinced that all the movie heros are in the audience.'"

"He told W.C. Fields, 'Your ninety-proof breath could start a windmill in an old Dutch painting. If I put a wick in you, you would burn for three years.'"

One Miznerite, Jimmy Irving recalls, "Although Wilson's health deteriorated in his last years, his wit which was widely known from his pauses in the wilds of the Yukon to salons of aristocratic Palm Beach, never abated. His diverse personalities were evident from his explanation in answer to Jimmy Cagney's curiosity that he got his broken knuckles from slugging broads in the Yukon'...to the role that William Powell played as a suave and sophisticated outlaw in ONE WAY PASSAGE."

Less publicized was the kindness and spirit of helpfulness of Mizner to his cronies and friends...which belied his razor-keen tongue. Broadway's and Hollywood's bitterest cynic was also its easiest "touch".

In his final days, weakened by a severe bout with a cold and confined to his bed, he had a sinking spell and the house physician, Dr. Bak and a priest were hastily summoned.

Mrs. Bak tells it. Mizner opened his eyes and painfully said to the priest. "I've been talking to your boss, Father." The priest smiled "don't be facetious, Wilson, you might have only a few more hours to live." "What!", answered the sick man, "No two-weeks notice?"

Mizner had his two weeks, then died on April 3, 1933 not without having the last word. Before he lost consciousness he took Dr. Bak's hand, smiled, and said "So long Doc, I guess this is the Main Event."

Even though Drs. Felger and Bak were the house doctors, prominent physician Joe Zeiler practised in the neighborhood and frequently stayed in the hotel. Often, as a favor, he would accomodate a guest that he knew, but on one occasion he did not know the patient, and the generous man couldn't refuse to help.

He and his friend Bill Jasper were having lunch at Perino's before going to a S.C. football game when Dr. Joe was called to the telephone by Goldy, the hotel switchboard operator.

"Even on the telephone," related Jasper, "Zeiler diagnosed the trouble as appendecitis and agreed to perform the surgery, then immediately ordered an ambulance to pick up the patient and meet him at the hospital.

"The patient got along very well, and later called Zeiler saying that he had received the doctor's bill for $150...but it did not seem sufficient and that he would send him a check for $1,000. Zeiler refused, and the patient said he would instead send him something from New York when he got home. The *something* turned out to be a stock certificate...with a caution not to sell it until he told him to. Several months later, Joe got a call about the certificate...which he had almost forgotten... with the order to 'SELL.'"

And sell he did...for $103,000.

Some fee.

The "King" Clark Gable and his "Queen" Carole Lombard bundled up at a sports event.

# Good Sports

Early Lido Pool photo.

Sports and leisure time, as in all of Southern California have ever been important to the Ambassador way of life.

The outdoor swimming pool is noted for its cabanas, fun and frolic. Early on, sand created a beach at one end, and a great bath house with steam rooms, exercise equipment and massages provided other luxuries.

Film star residents and wintering guests frequented the pool regularly. Expensive, private home pools were to come later when stars built their mansions, but here poolside entertaining was informal and popular. Ruby Keeler lived at the hotel, and often Al Jolson with his buddies, Eddie Cantor, Ben Bernie and Walter Winchell would roll out a piano, sing songs and entertain. At times it got pretty lively with everyone getting into the act... and into the pool... with and without swim suits.

Long time resident and prominent Doctor, Jack Murrieta was one of the neighborhood kids who played around the construction of the hotel. "When the building was completed and the pool was added, we felt it was ours. Most of the kids in the neighborhood took swim lessons, many later competing in tournaments.

"We were often treated to exhibitions by the superb athletes of the day. It was exciting to watch the professionals, Olive Hatch, Duke Kahanamoku and Johnny Weismuller compete. In fact, the Ambassador pool very likely contributed to the great interest in swimming competition in California. Jackie Coogan took lessons with us too...he lived just down the street. A lot of those very kids are now doctors, lawyers and bankers...still living in this same area."

Recently, a guest of the hotel was the first to hit the pool every morning. He was staying at the hotel for the Academy of Science and Fiction Award's Presentation program which he was to MC for television, by invitation of its president, Dr. Ronald Reed.

Presently living in Arizona, the swimmer remarked he had been looking forward to his visit, and the pool, as it was where he had arduously trained for the 1932 Olympics. His name? Buster Crabbe aka... Tarzan, Buck Rogers and Flash Gordon.

A miniature golf course (with its own golf pro!) at one time wrapped itself around the hotel...and frequently guests could watch notables such as Howard Hughes and Marion Davies practising early mornings before taking off for Rancho or Wilshire Country Club. Today, a putting course remains...and it is bordered by a jogging track.

FIVE JUNIOR SWIM CHAMPS

# *Smart Set Will Occupy Horse Show Boxes*

## *Aristocrats Will Don Gala Attire for Affair*

*A remarkable flashlight of the great Ambassador Horse Show Arena.* Keystone Phot

Horse shows for the society and horsey set were spectacular affairs.

Beginning in 1921 and continuing for several years annual horse shows were de rigueur.

Headlines heralded: BLUE BLOODS FROM ALL PARTS OF AMERICA TO TAKE PART IN BIG SOCIAL AND EQUINE EVENT.

Quoting from CALIFORNIA OUTDOORS AND IN, "Los Angeles and nearby society will again turn its attention to the Ambassador Hotel Auditorium for the opening of this year's Annual Los Angeles Horse Show and its brilliant exhibition of America's equine aristocracy."

Usually, at least 115 ring events with approximately 300 horses (including saddle and harness horses and ponies, polo mounts, hunter and jumpers), of highest show rating competed for at least $40,000 in cash prizes. In addition, many championship cups and trophies were awarded. Held in winter, Eastern entries were numerous, welcomed by them "to test the quality of Eastern horses against California's best", and probably to escape the cold weather. Spectacular equestrian activities were featured including series of jumping contests for U.S. Army officers, and competitors from the fashionable Marlborough girls school.

Said one writer of the third show, "This great annual mid-winter affair, so attractive to resident and visiting society, will include a greater number of social and equine features and reach greater spectacular heights than ever before. From the side of its social significance, the outstanding feature yearly is the Horse Show Ball in the Cocoanut Grove, it being the purpose of Show directors to include additional social objectives and gaieties."

California society as well was represented as William Matson Roth of San Francisco recalled that both he and his mother participated...their stable being one of California's largest. Southern Californian participants and box-holders "was the social register laid out before your eyes." To name a few. Ben Myer, Cecilia deMille, Irving Hellman, the Bixbys, Brants, Barnes, Bullocks, Burks, Bells, Clarkes, DeMonds, Fuquas, Fertigs, Garlands, Hellmans, Haldemans, Hancocks, etc. (You'll note the alphabetical order. The columnist didn't show status or preference).

*Miss Jane Woodin with Mr. Guy Woodin and Trainer. The Woodins are ranked among Southern California's best riders and will take part in the forthcoming show at The Ambassador.*

TWO CHAMPIONS . . . Britain's top equestrienne Anneli Drummond-Hay putting California champion, I'm A Clown, through his paces on the Ambassador lawn.

# Californians Hold Tennis Laurels

Ben Gorchakoff — May Sutton Bundy — Bill Tilden

Tennis was as spectacular and as socially noblesse oblige.

And that's why any deviation or aberration in the game or by the players sent shocks through the whole city, reaching throughout the world.

Ben Gorchakoff was well known as a tennis instructor for the Ambassador Hotel Courts, bringing championship quality, excitement, dignity...along with a lovely wife and two children...to the courts and to the game.

He remembered, "California rose to the uppermost pinnacle in the realm of tennis and became the leading producer of tennis champions. Playing in competition on our courts were all the greatest of tennis aces: Ellsworth Vines, Mrs. Helen Wills Moody, Gene Mako, Bunny Ryan, Johnny Van Ryn, Lester Stoefen, Jack Tidball, Ruby Bishop, Don Budge, Fred Perry, Keith Gledhill and May Sutton Bundy."

Sportlite Publications claimed, "Ben Gorchakoff is proving to be one of the most popular players ever to appear. He endears himself to the gallery from the first moment that he sets foot upon the court. He is a crowd pleaser at all times with his hard hitting, rough and ready game of dash and vigor. Pleasing is the manner in which he storms the net. Win or lose, his supporters love him." The article in explaining a player, also indicates the emotion and esteem in which the game is held.

Champions played and partied with a Hollywood crowd, who were both players and audience. Faithful to the game, the stars could be found with socialites bunched in wooden bleachers with men wearing (regardless of the heat of the day) gray flannel suits and ladies with furs over long white dresses. Silver trophies were used for champagne ladling, and epicurean food was served al fresco on expensive china.

Some of the box-holders were the Haldemans, whose son was to work for Richard Nixon, the Janss family, who conceived Westwood, and developers of Bel Air, Alphonzo Bell Sr., the U. S. Congressman's father, Secretary of State under President Wilson, and Harvey Mudd, who had a college named after him.

Never to miss tournaments were Charles Chaplin, Gary Cooper, Clark Gable, Jack Benny, Spencer Tracy, Boris Karloff, Samuel Goldwyn, Ozzie and Harriet, and Actor/Senator George Murphy.

The hotel was headquarters for most players competing in the Pacific Southwest tournaments. Memorable were some of the humorous events. Frenchman Henri Cochet, still in bed when notified it was time to play, informed the tournament director that he never played before 2 P.M.

Dr. Gerald Bartosh, a friendly, local doctor, often treated players for ailments. Although he was competing in a set of quarter-finals...he treated Donald

Budge for a sprained neck before he was to face him on the court. "Although," the Times reported, "The good doctor wasn't obligated to get Budge back in shape...he was a good Samaritan, anyway, and see what he got...a three-set licking."

But there was no humor in the declining career of "Big Bill" Tilden, the greatest of them all.

"He was an artist," Franklin P. Adams wrote of him. "*The* ranking tennis player in the world...it is the beauty of the game that Tilden loves; it is the chase always, rather than the quarry." Later the words "chase" and "quarry" would have another meaning. Tilden, a Philadelphia socialite, loved the good life. It was known at the Ambassador where he headquartered, that he enjoyed playing bridge (he was a master) was a connoisseur of fine music and was well-read. As his biographer Frank Deford said, "he held pretensions to writing and acting as well as tennis, but these gossamer vanities only cost him great amounts of stature and money, and even held him up to mockery." Admired by the movie colony he was in great demand at parties and tennis matches held on private courts, particularly at his friend Charlie Chaplin's house, where he would play with Gussie Moran, and other of his students and friends, Greta Garbo, Errol Flynn, Joseph Cotten, Tallulah Bankhead, Spencer Tracy, Olivia de Havilland, Farley Granger and Shelley Winters...and they would all respond with attending his tougher matches on the Ambassador and Los Angeles Tennis Club courts.

Though surrounded by admiring friends, "Big Bill" could not make real friends of either sex. Instead he sought the company of young boys, driven by the searcl. .o find in one the son and successor he could never have. Primarily asexual when his star began to fade and he lost the emotional uplift that crowd worship provided, his homosexual proctivities revealed themselves. It was the beginning of the end.

Jackie Coogan recently related that he was allowed to watch Tilden play on the Ambassador courts, but never unchaperoned when he was a young boy. Frank Deford tells of Tilden's coaching Adela Rogers St. John's young son Dick, who became one of his better students.

Adela, the Hearst reporter who had known "Big Bill" for years and played foursomes with him, Howard Hughes and Douglas Fairbanks, had a no-nonsense relationship with him. Asking Tilden to be her son's coach, she extracted a flat-out promise from him that he would keep his hands off the boy. Under Tilden's tutelage, Dick improved steadily and went on to win junior championships.

Indicted and serving time on the second occasion for "lewd and lascivious behavior with a minor", it was on his release that he learned Associated Press had named him the "greatest athlete of the half-century." He was the only hold-over in the sports world from that Golden Era, when Jack Dempsey, Babe Ruth, Red Grange, Johnny Weismuller, Charley Paddock and Bobby Jones were the ruling champions. He was still winning tournaments while they were retiring. The first "showman" of the tennis world, he dominated the game for years.

Tilden, the champion, was strong and invincible in his professional life...

Tilden, the man, weak, and sadly vulnerable in his personal life.

Watching the pros: Marlene Dietrich and her daughter, and Bing and Dixie Crosby.

Buster Crabbe used the Lido pool to practice for the Olympics, but recently told us that a photo taken of him at the pool holding a cigarette lost the trip for him. Handsome, virile and talented, Buster was soon spotted for motion pictures, and has had a long and rewarding career as an actor.

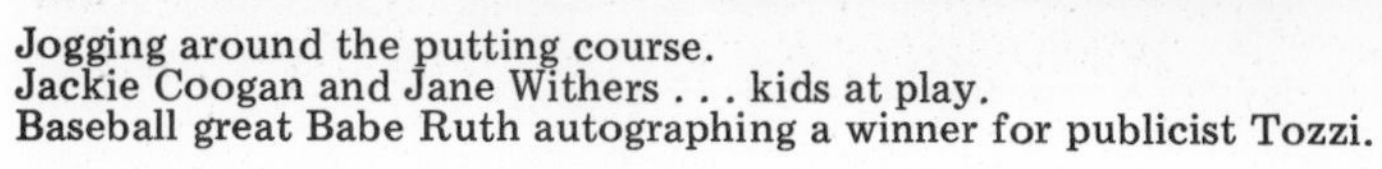

Jogging around the putting course.
Jackie Coogan and Jane Withers . . . kids at play.
Baseball great Babe Ruth autographing a winner for publicist Tozzi.

**Championship pool and tennis courts today. The lawn does get a work-out. Exhibit put on by two boxers headed for a fight at the Forum. They arrived by helicopter to make it even more visual and exciting.**

# Politics and Bedlam

President Lyndon Johnson.

"Hostess with the mostest" Perle Mesta with Mrs. Johnson and daughter Linda Bird.
Vice President and Mrs. Hubert Humphrey.
President Herbert Hoover with U.S. Ambassador Dawes.

No records are around reflecting just when the Ambassador became a force in the political arena, but history does relate that while visiting Los Angeles in 1920, a young man on a Navy inspection tour drove by the site of the emerging hotel, and commented to friends that he would come back some day to register in the Presidential Suite.

His name? Franklin Delano Roosevelt.

Presidents from Hoover, Roosevelt, Truman, Eisenhower (as a young soldier), Kennedy, Johnson, and Nixon headquartered at the hotel...often at the same time.

Veterans of, and newcomers on the campaign trails, headquartered at the hotel. It was the favored California meeting place for secretive or ballyhooed confabs of Republicans, Democrats and Independent parties.

Here Hubert Humphrey charmed his constituents; Nelson Rockefeller was enthusiastically supported; Ronald Reagan raised vast sums with the help of movie buddies; Lyndon Johnson playfully, crudely patted female reporters and maids on their derrieres...and the world heard the press being told, "You won't have Nixon to kick around any more."

President and Mrs. Richard Nixon.
President Nixon and Tray Burk.

Ambassador Philip Weber with
President and Mrs. Richard Nixon.

I recalled that episode recently when I had occasion to visit with the former president at his home in San Clemente, and asked if his memories of the Ambassador were sad ones. "No," he answered, "I have some wonderful memories of the hotel. I spent a great deal of time with good friends at the Ambassador." And the hotel remembers much planning and campaign strategy that took place with high placed officials and Republican supporters for Nixon.

In 1948 the hotel informed President Harry Truman that trade unions were having a dispute, and that for his pending visit where he was to be the speaker and guest of the Greater Los Angeles Press Club's luncheon at the hotel, he might be faced with crossing a picket line. Fortunately, a settlement was reached, so that he would not be embarrassed. The staff remembers his visit well. The President, Mrs. Truman with their daughter Margaret, aides and security took one whole floor for their accommodations. Everyone was impressed with the First Family's pleasantness and consideration...especially one valet delivering laundry to the President. Truman asked him, "Haven't I met you somewhere before?" And before the valet could answer, he continued with..."of course, you worked at the Muehlbach in St. Louis!"

Honor, indignation and outrage accompanied the renowned visit of Premier Nikita Khrushchev. Both he and Russia were an enigma to the American people at the time, and the country was divided between extending a welcome, or renouncing his presence.

Many questioned the choice of the film colony when they entertained him and his wife on a movie set with a lively and somewhat tasteless live production of CAN-CAN. Mrs. Khrushchev especially seemed annoyed...but not nearly so as the Premier when he was refused a visit of Disneyland. He was not satisfied with the official explanation, that it was too much of a security risk.

The eyes of the world were on Khrushchev at the Ambassador at this time, and the hotel supplied phones...360 of them...and typewriters in news room facilities for reporters from all domestic and foreign newspapers and stations.

Ex-Governor Ronald Reagan and Nancy immediately after winning the California Republican nomination for President . . . at the Ambassador.

# Governors, Mayors and Diplomats...

Governor Ronald Reagan presenting the state flag to the Ambassador. Governor and Mrs. Goodwin Knight greeting Henry Cabot Lodge. Governor Pat Brown and Freddy Martin.

Singer Dennis Day with former California Governor, later Supreme Court Justice Earl Warren. Senator Edmund Muskie with newspaper editor Ed Duzik. Young California Governor Jerry Brown.

Maverick Mayor Sam Yorty. Former San Francisco Mayor Alioto. San Francisco Mayor George Mosconi who was slain in office. Secretary George Romney greeting friends at the Cocoanut Grove.

MB with Los Angeles Mayor Tom Bradley. A particularly interesting evening honoring Iranian Ambassador Ardeshir Zahedi, John Behjou and 98 other gentlemen with MB the only lady present. Enjoying a moment with Sam.

Aspirants to offices from local school boards (where and how Jerry Brown started) to Governor and President conduct campaigns, and have their victory parties or defeat wrap-ups in various ballrooms.

Vietnamese Vice President Ky holding a press conference. Ambassador Elliot Mizelle greeting German Chancellor Adenauer. Governor Reagan (soon to be President Reagan ) and Nancy.

Beautiful daughter of Spain's General Franco. Mrs. Martin Luther King at annual meeting with hundreds of her slain husband's devoted followers. One of hundreds of notable banquets . . . this famous moment with Russian Premier Nikita Khrushchev.

The first political dinner that I attended in the hotel was a fund-raiser for and by Democrats, as a guest of a friend, Congressman Cecil King. Prior to the dinner we visited California Governor Pat Brown in the Presidential Suite where we met young Robert Kennedy, brother of President John Kennedy, who was then Attorney General. Robert was the principal speaker of the evening...in the Embassy Ballroom.

I recall the intensity of the young man, seated at the head table beside his wife, taking notes as other speakers appeared, then kissing three of his children as they filed by him on their way to early bed.

But it was a later Bobby Kennedy appearance in the same ballroom, very nearly on the same spot...more notable and lamentable...that affected the whole world, and certainly the future of this nation.

Political parties and staffs often took up residence for months at a time while plotting and running campaigns...and it was such a purpose that brought the Robert Kennedy party to the hotel in mid-March, 1968.

Living had not been very light-hearted in the sixties. Civil rights protagonists were marching, ghettos burned in Cleveland and Chicago; riots broke out in black communities throughout the nation; while casualty lists mounted in Vietnam in a war that many fighting it seemed to think had no purpose.

It was the age of the flower child, youth trips and communal living. Youths were confused and rejecting parents...many becoming drug users, and some psychotic. Psychedelia and nudity became popular. Miniskirts and hot pants were the fad; rock and roll was the rage, and the world of music was seized by the phenomenon called the "Beatles."

This was the decade when crazed individuals snuffed out the lives of the country's leaders. President Kennedy in 1963, Martin Luther King in 1968 to be followed a scant two months later by the man many referred to as "ruthless" while even seasoned reporters "found it so easy to fall in love with", Bobby Kennedy.

The Kennedy men were no strangers to the Ambassador. Both Robert and John had attended Democratic functions, and John had participated in a romantic pause or two in the hotel. "Founding Father" Joseph, in his multiple business dealings of cornering the scotch market, amassing millions in New York real estate and dealing with oil interests necessary to the World War effort, had also taken a hand in the glamorous film business in Hollywood. And partnered with the most glamorous of them all, Gloria Swanson. And so the younger Kennedys were no strangers to Hollywood and became familiar with filmdom and its stars early on.

Records revive visits of John, one by helicopter, and a few arriving and leaving by a clandestine entrance...and several visits over the years by Bobby, usually accompanied by political aides, and frequently by his wife Ethel and some of their numerous children.

President Sekou Joure of Guinea with Ambassador Harry Jenkinson. Korean President Synghman Rhee and his First Lady. Senator George Murphy, David Eisenhower (grandson of President Eisenhower and son-in-law of President Nixon) with Ambassador's Franz Stalpers and MB.

# Death of A Hero

A beaming Bobby Kennedy on the night of June 5,1968, accepts the victory cheers from the jammed-in-crowd in the Ambassador Hotel Ballroom. 'On to Chicago,' he said, as he left the podium by way of the kitchen where Sirhan was waiting to assassinate him.

Enthusiastic staff members and energetic volunteers prepared the way for Bobby to win the California Democratic Presidential primary.

The candidate had been stampeding across the nation for weeks with inordinate speed, to catch up with the days that had been lost due to his late uncharacteristic seizure of caution in announcing his decision to be a candidate for the office of President.

On Sunday before the California primary, Kennedy had appeared before groups in the hotel, and addressed other wild and enthusiastic supporters in the green and flowery East gardens. It was during this period that he rejected, then heatedly dismissed the protection of the Los Angeles Police Department.

Frequently during his Ambassador stay, Kennedy was seen by the hotel staff alone, walking his dog in the gardens without his own security...which was frustrating and worrisome to them.

Then the party flew to San Francisco for appearances, back from San Francisco to Long Beach, through Watts and Venice, then again boarding a plane for San Diego and the El Cortez Hotel where celebrities Andy Williams and Rosemary Clooney would entertain on his behalf. He was exhausted and not feeling well... as he had appeared and admitted to his entourage.

The following day was June 4...election day. A day off, at least until late afternoon when sample precinct reports from California would come in. So the Kennedys decided to spend the night and the next day at John Frankenheimer's beach house in Malibu with six of their children.

On this, the last day of his life, he slept late, had lunch, then took to the beach with the kids. It was chilly and overcast but he plunged into the waves anyway. Suddenly, he spied 12 year old David being pulled down by an undertow. He dove in and came up with the boy, and a red bruise on his own forehead.

He returned to the hotel shortly after 7 P.M. to his Royal Suite accommodations to find them filled with 100 of his staff, some privileged reporters and other hangers-on. Several television, radio and newspaper interviews with the Senator followed while they all watched the returns on television.

With him were many of those closest to both Bobby and John: Ethel; sister Jean and her husband, Stephen Smith; Pierre Salinger (formerly Jack's press officer); Fred Dutton; Ted Sorenson; Rosey Grier; Olympic decathalon champ, Rafer Johnson; author Theodore White; Budd Schulberg; George Plimpton; and the first American astronaut to orbit the earth, John Glenn. All of the faces were happy. Mother Rose had been registered in the hotel, but left sometime previous to this night. Reservations indicated that a reservation had been made for Jackie Onassis, but not picked up by her.

The Kennedy children, David, Michael, Courtney and Kerry were there with him too.

When both CBS and NBC forecast that Kennedy was winning the California primary election over Senator Eugene McCarthy, press officer Frank Mankiewicz rushed in to Kennedy's bedroom where he was hunched on the edge of the bed, tired, edgy, looking small and vulnerable. His son David kissed him on the cheek and sat down close to his father.

Mankiewicz urged him to hurry saying that a more-than-capacity crowd of 1,800 were waiting. Kennedy turned to where Ethel, pregnant with their 11th child was resting. "Ready?" he asked. "Ready!" she answered, rising brightly.

It was about 15 minutes before midnight when Kennedy came down the service elevator and through the hotel kitchen. He shook hands with kitchen workers and walked through the service areas to the Embassy where he was received in the brilliantly lit-for-television ballroom by screaming, touching, joyous celebrating Californians.

For several minutes he spoke jovially, congratulating Los Angeles Dodger Don Drysdale on pitching his sixth straight shutout that night, and said "I hope that we have as good fortune in our campaign." He thanked his supporters and the men running his campaign, Cesar Chavez; Jesse Unruh; Paul Schrade; Rafer Johnson; Rosie Grier; his dog Freckles, and last but not least his wife Ethel. Then he gave his victory talk, and ended with his political aims and thanking "all of you who made this evening possible."

Pandemonium broke loose as Kennedy reached out to shake hands with the cheering and applauding mob. Hundreds of flash bulbs were popping, and television cameras were turning.

He turned to leave, hesitated for a brief moment, then chose a direction *opposite* the original plan. He was to have gone *west* down a back stairwell to another reception in the convention area of the lower Casino level, but his aides Fred Dutton and Bill Barry decided that those functionaries had seen it all on closed circuit television, and because it was past midnight, the writing newsmen were pushing deadlines, Kennedy should first see them.

So as Barry told him: "We're going this way," they started *east* down the side steps that lead onto the ballroom floor from the stage, and then directly out into the kitchen corridor through the swinging doors used by waiters serving the room, to the Colonial Room via its back door which also led off the kitchen/pantry corridor. But Kennedy was not following.

Kennedy, boxed in by reaching, screaming well-wishers chanting "We want Bobby!" was not able to keep up with them, so he took Assistant maitre d'hotel Karl Uecker's hand, and they both followed hotel executive Uno Timanson through the gold curtains *behind* the rostrum which guided the Senator off the rear of the platform directly through the double doors leading to the same pantry corridor.

Kennedy stopped by the large ice-making machine and service tables, shaking hands with members of the kitchen staff.

Struggling through the crowd to reach him were Mrs. Kennedy and several aides who had been separated by the change of course.

He turned to look for Ethel while he was answering a question of Mutual Radio reporter, Andrew West when, witnesses report, a single soft "pop", followed by a rapid volley of repeated "pops" sounded. Hotel employee Jesus Perez testified before the grand jury, "I was shaking hands with him, and then he let go and fell to the floor."

Kennedy's hands went up toward his face. The impact threw his arms over his head, his feet were apart and he was lying about two feet from the side of the ice machine on the cold, grey floor. He was mortally wounded by the gun of Jordanian immigrant Sirhan Sirhan. He was barely alive.

His eyes were open, but he could not see William Weisel, Ira Goldstein, Elizabeth Evans, Irwin Stroll and Paul Schrade in the split seconds following...falling behind him from the same assassin's bullets.

As Uecker and banquet captain Edward Minasian grabbed the hand holding the gun, Bill Barry swung at the man while Rosey Grier and Rafer Johnson were reaching to pin him down.

Vincent De Pierro, a 19 year old college freshman working as a waiter that night told the Grand Jury that he saw Sirhan point the gun, and pull the trigger.

Young kitchen worker, Juan Romero, knelt at the side of Kennedy, wrapped a rosary around Kennedy's left thumb and folded his hand over it. Kennedy brought the rosary up to his chest while Romero cradled his head and whispered, "Come on, Mr. Kennedy...you can make it."

Several minutes passed before Mrs. Kennedy, who had been pulled back to safety when the gunfire broke out, now was brought forward.

According to reporter Jules Witcover's version, she came up behind where her husband lay, but because of the crowd and the bedlam she did not see him until she was at his head. Tenderly she took his hand. He turned his head and seemed to recognize her. She knelt there, in her orange and white party dress, on both knees, stooped low over the cold concrete floor, whispering to him, stroking his bare chest and brow. His last words to her were, "Am I alright?"

Mrs. Kennedy, her face full of anguish and pleading, but without tears and under control, rose and turned to those nearby, "Please go, please go. Give him room to breathe," she said.

Edward Minasian made the emergency call and at 12:23 A.M., six minutes later, the ambulance arrived.

Soon after he was strapped onto the stretcher, Bobby Kennedy lost consciousness. As he was being carried...again on a freight elevator to the waiting ambulance...Juan Romero took a white towel and began to mop up the pool of blood that had formed under his head.

As the nation waited for reports on Senator Kennedy's condition, the television networks continued to show reruns of the bizarre scene in the Ambassador kitchen.

With his family and those friends and supporters close to him anguishing on the fifth floor of the Good Samaritan Hospital, knowing that it could not be much longer, the brain of Robert Francis Kennedy died on June 5 at 6:30 P.M., and his body followed at 1:44 A.M. on June 6, 1968...25½ hours after the shooting. He was 42 years old.

It was cruel. It was a disaster, a needless one. Still unsolved in the minds of many...perhaps as many different versions as were people there, the assassination has been reenacted in the kitchen, in dozens of books and in hundreds of meetings and conversations. It is considered "The case that won't close".

But the final chapter of Robert Kennedy's life, perhaps even a prediction, might be found in the poem by his favorite poet Aeschylus that he was fond of quoting:

*"In our sleep, pain which cannot forget*
*Falls drop by drop upon the heart until,*
*In our own despair...against our will...*
*Comes wisdom through the awful grace of God."*

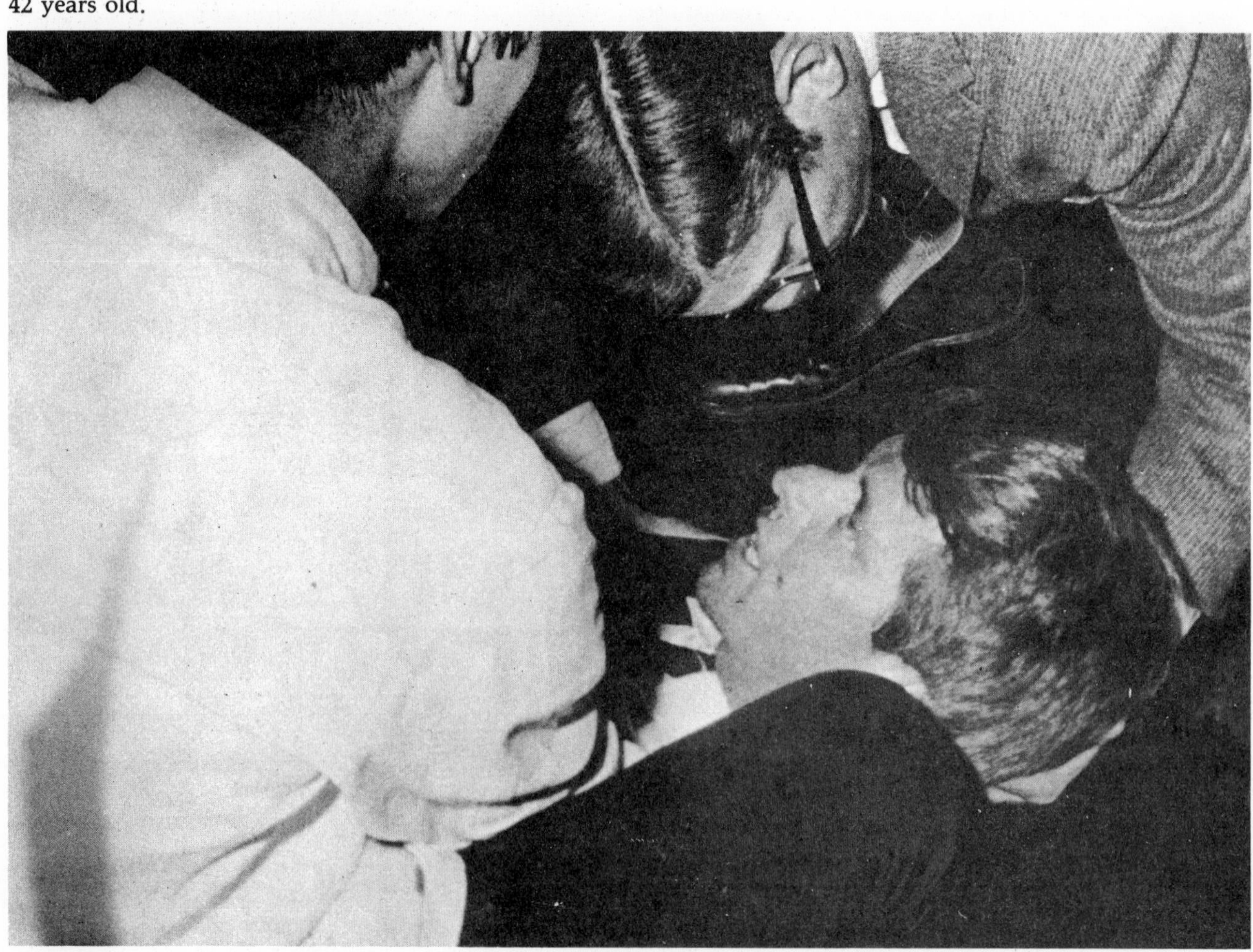

**Bobby Kennedy tries to speak as he lies wounded. He was shot in the head moments after making his victory speech to his supporters in the Embassy Ballroom.**

Columnist Walter Winchell, a regular and frequent guest of the hotel was usually in residence during political events. He told this story in his autobiography which was released after his death.

"When Senator Barry Goldwater was competing for the Presidential primaries in 1964, I ran a newspaper poll: GOLDWATER OR JOHNSON? Readers were invited to mail in a postcard with the name of the candidate they wanted to win.

"The cards came in bundles, most of them from Southern California Republicans and from the six states that Goldwater later won for President. Very few cards mentioned LBJ. As the poll indicated, Goldwater won the primary in California.

"When Johnson and Goldwater were nominated, I repeated the poll. Goldwater's crowd sent cards, many with the same handwriting—but different names. One afternoon the cashier in the barbershop at J. Myer Schine's Hotel Ambassador (Los Angeles) announced, You have a call from the White House. Landlord Schine, getting a shave, was impressed.

I took the call. The caller said, "My name is Busby, White House. Please hold—a friend wants to talk to you."

Hello, Walter, said another voice.

Who you? I asked.

Lyndon Johnson.

Hi, Mister Pressadint! I ejaculated. What have I done now?

How'm ah doin'? he asked softly.

How do you mean, Mr. President?

How'm ah doin' with your silly poll?

I'm cutting it out at once. I found out they were stacking the cards. They contact Republican Clubs and suggest members shower me with postcard votes for Goldwater. Stupid. Tomorrow I'm printing the reason I am stopping it.

How do you think I will come out? the President asked.

I wish I knew. May I suggest you contact your leaders and—

My Whaaaatttt? LBJ interrupted.

Your leaders!

My leaders? he shouted, Ahm the leadahhhh!

"The patrons in the barbershop, who could hear him, rocked with laughter, too."

Soon after, Winchell met Goldwater.

"The protection for Barry Goldwater by San Francisco lawmen was so tight that when I tried to get through the crowd waiting to see the candidate and his wife get into their limousine his top aides said, "Nobody! Nobody!" Top GOPeople came along and okayed it.

"Earlier that week in Los Angeles, as Mr. Goldwater and aides (one was L.A. Sheriff Peter Pitchess) got into the Hotel Ambassador elevator to go up to Goldwater's suites on the fifth floor, I was stopped by a hotel security officer when I pushed my way in with them.

"Sheriff Pitchess okayed me. He introduced me to Mr. Goldwater.

"When we got out on the fifth floor the Sheriff (a former G-man) said: "Why don't you get to know each other?"

"Goldwater said: Why don't you like me?

I don't dislike you, Senator, I'm a Democrat.

On another political occasion:

"At the Los Angeles Hotel Ambassador when Southern California Democrats hosted a fund-raising affair, newspaper people were not permitted near the entrance to the same Embassy Room where Senator Kennedy was later shot. I had been invited by Demo chiefs to join them at a table close to where LBJ would make a speech. I elected to remain with my colleagues but refused to be confined in the Colonial Room nearby. I live here, I told a Secret Service man.

"He apparently was ordered to stand in front of me—belly to belly. Frank Sinatra came out to go to the washroom, I started over to speak with Frank but was surrounded by agents who barred the way. Along came Gov. Pat Brown with LBJ's then press chief, George Reedy. I told them at least one reporter and news photographer should be permitted in the big ballroom in case something happens. No dice.

"That's the way to *protect* a President.

Famous columnist Walter Winchell. This was the last photo ever taken of him. He died while a resident of the hotel. MB witnessed his last will and testament.

Dawn and haze are abreast in their rise to meet the new day... and a greyness unknown to early California prevails. Slowly, even as one watches, the sun rays move ahead burning through the fuzzy blanket, and the yellow brilliance, strong reds, cool greens, sky blues and mauves native to California alone shine out to greet the visitor.

The giant hotel stirs itself awake in the evolving of a new day. Baby grass seedlings peek up through the new putting green turf, rainbow-hued, dewy-fresh blossoms stand delicate guard around acres of grassy lawn and spit-polished guest bungalows, while silver streaks of refreshing water whirly bird a tune to which early walkers dodge and dance.

A lone grey garbed shapeless figure pants around the modish jogging track, inhaling/exhaling the fresh morning scents, while other hardy early morning risers with gear over their arms head for the tennis courts and swimming pool.

Small clusters of employees in spotless starched uniforms, minutes before clocking in, clucking with one another in muted tones...some reliving last night... others probably dissecting the "bosses."

Night people summing up, cleaning up, catching up, waking up... taking off.

A general feeling of business...the self contained city girdles for the day.

Maids silently re-making the beds...impatient for adjacent rooms to empty and get them through their chores a "little earlier today."

An army of vacuums being driven through the myriad of halls, erasing yesterday's signs.

In the bakery, men in white, topping custard tarts with fresh dewy strawberries, and building Napoleons for guests to topple with eager forks at lunch. Chef-hatted, not-for-long crispy-white uniformed cooks framed by stainless steel kitchens standing over steaming, mammoth cauldrons building meals for millions.

Brillo pads attacking giant dishwashers before receiving tons of food-ladened rejects to bring them back to their snowy whiteness...again.

Sheepish expressioned electrician encased in his tool belt, sitting squatty Indian-fashion in the center of the emptied foyer fountain, commenting "first they want it lit, then they don't."

Serious, but not yet wide awake room clerks checking in, checking out swarms of impatient faces, while bellmen wrestle assorted Gucci and Samsonite luggage, rope tied boxes, shapeless plastic hangered best clothes and Disneyland Mickeymice and hats.

A couple with sorrow in their faces, arms around each other's waists, saying goodbye...oblivious to the people and the hub-bub.

Dozens of sleepy-eyed-look-alike lucky teenagers, preparing for the onslaught through the city and to the movie studios, on the grand tour furnished by generous parents who can't move most of them from their vacation beds before noon at home.

Outwardly, the appearance of the Ambassador, as with most hotels, is of constant change. Its pulse-rate is rapid; instantaneous and flashing are the patterns of movement, and the succeeding sea of coming and going faces become one big blur...except in the case of some permanent residents who have found it a comfortable, roomy and warm place to live.

From early days when one could observe "family" John Barrymore feeding his monkey; Pola Negri walking her cheetah; and Gloria Swanson entertaining in the gardens at tea-time; Howard Hughes practise-putting on the lawn; Walter Winchell gathering tid-bits for his column; to Robert Kennedy early-morning jogging, and my poodle Amy Semple McBurk mushing through the ivy, the Ambassador has been home for lengthy periods to many residents. From Churchill, Einstein, the Armours, Vanderbilts, Du Ponts to a Thai Prince; stars Chaplin, Monroe, Davies, Goudal; members of the Counsulor Corps while finding their own homes; to members of the Press, new to Los Angeles searching for theirs, to attorney Mark Cohen who like Winchell was a resident for over 50 years, and Joe Weisfelt beginning in 1928 who still is...the Ambassador has spelled home. To say nothing of Mickey Cohen and many of his hood cowarts, and various other gangsters during the bootlegging days.

## Intriguing Family

Long-time resident Joe Weisfelt with the very charming Mrs. Myer Shine.

This "cast" of the Ambassador and the stories they relate would require another book, but I can't resist a few samples.

Famous evangelist Aimee Semple McPherson maintained a suite, which was veiled in secrecy. It was the only place she could "relax" with friends, and others with whom she shared greater intimacies, but not with her colleagues who were unaware of where she slipped off to. A few hotel maids knew where Aimee was part of the time when she was supposed to have been "kidnapped" and ultimately surfaced (after a disappearing act) in Carmel with a lover.

✶✶✶✶

Although she considered herself clairvoyant, writer Elinor Glyn never was able to clarify the mystery that revealed itself when she heard a shot and scuffles outside her parlor where she was entertaining Marion Davies and Charlie Chaplin. Opening the door she saw a man lying on the floor in the hallway. He had been shot, and his assassin was standing over him with a smoking revolver. Running up behind them were several policemen who had been in hot pursuit of the man with the gun. They admonished Elinor and her friends to "Get back in that room!", which they did. Not a word was in the morning paper about the murder...So Elinor immediately dressed and called on the hotel manager.

"What shots? What murder? What gunman?" was the position of the puzzled (?) manager.

★★★★

Everyone felt the sorrow Sid Grauman suffered upon the loss of his mother. But it reached morbid proportions, when for months he admonished maids to leave her room untouched where the usually fun loving man would brood by the hour.

"Come sit with me," and who could resist Maurice Chevalier?

Author Elinor Glyn with one of her story-book characters.

On a recent visit to Los Angeles, petite and brilliant Anita Loos, author of GENTLEMEN PREFER BLONDES, who when she was in her teens became one of moviedom's earliest script writers, passed by the still-elegant Talmadge apartment building a block from the hotel which had been a gift to Norma Talmadge from her husband Joe Schenck. It set her to reminiscing about the Talmadge sisters who had been her very close friends. Joe Schenck had married the beautiful and sultry actress Norma and while previously a wealthy and successful theatre chain owner, had entered into the production of movies only for the purpose of furthering the career of his wife, whom he had "rescued from obscurity" and married. The films he produced for her established her as the foremost dramatic star of silents.

Along with her sister Constance, the two girls became well-known stars of their day, but Peg their mother...a real movie-mother, one whom everyone loved because of her earthiness and ribald sense of humor, according to Anita, "never allowed success to go to her daughter's heads. Her stock admonition was, 'Now girls, don't get the idea you're important because you make faces in front of a camera.' "

Even though Peg had raised her girls alone, through great hardships and deprivation, she adored them. But of one occasion Anita recalled, "Peg always made fun of herself as relentlessly as she did of her daughters. We decided to give Peg a birthday party in their luxurious five-room suite at the Ambassador. That day we barged into Peg's bedroom to surprise her with gifts, of which those from Norma and Dutch were very expensive costumes. While contemplating her loot, Peg began to laugh. 'What's the joke, Peg?' Norma asked. 'It's a joke on me,' she said. 'I just remembered how I used to go to Coney Island before you were born and ride that bumpy roller coaster, trying to lose you rich little bastards.' "

"Dearest Dear: Unfortunately this is the only way to make good the frightful wrong I have done you and to wipe out my abject humiliation. I love you. Paul (P.S.) You understand that last night was only a comedy", was the suicide note left to Jean Harlow upon the death of her husband, MGM producer, Paul Bern. It is difficult to realize that this much publicized and remembered case occured almost 50 years ago...and that the couple were married for only two months before Bern's alleged suicide took place. As with Marilyn Monroe, there are many interpretations as to the cause of his death, some negating suicide.

MGM leaked the rumor that Bern was impotent and suffered from infantile genitalia, thus the meaning of the suicide note. Others insist that in truth, Bern had a common law wife, actress Dorothy Millette, confined to a sanitarium in Connecticut at the time he married Harlow, and when she left the sanitarium and threatened to visit Bern in Hollywood, he shot himself. Reason? He did not want to drag any of the parties into what he felt would become a messy and sensational suit. Rumors were rampant. It was believed that "Harlow was with him when he shot himself," "someone else shot him," amongst other opinions...but residents of the Ambassador, where Bern had lived for several years before his marriage, were puzzled about something the general public did not know. Bern visited the hotel the afternoon of his death, arriving and spending the day with a young lady in a bungalow under an assumed name.

Prior to their marriage, Jean, because of her screen image, suffered from a bad, but inappropriate reputation which made her appear to be a hot sex object. In fact, she was intelligent, friendly, warm...dearly loved by cast and crews with whom worked. Affectionately, she was called "Baby" by her friends, but her roles of trollop, gangster's moll, prostitute and vulgar comedienne, along with her platinum hair, beautiful face and perfect body portrayed her as little more than a dumb, oversexed bleached blond. An impression that was utterly confounding and distressing to her. However, with time she became more popular and obtained roles of sophistication, humor and dignity, and became a star of first magnitude...capable of having almost any man she desired.

Harlow's public was astounded and not a little disappointed when she married Bern, who was a small, not-very-attractive man who seemingly was no match for the beautiful star. She explained to her friend Adela Rogers St. Johns that she had chosen Paul because he was sweet to her, loving, and interested in her career...and not only in her body or in the phony symbol she had become.

Jetta Goudal, protegee of Cecil B. DeMille and star of many early films, herself called "that consummate she-devil of the silent screen" was a resident of the hotel at that time. She explains Bern. "He was a friend and advisor to many of us who were new and alone in the film business. He was most intellectual, a successful producer, and was considered a connoisseur of beauty. A trustworthy man, he was one of the few who didn't try to force the sex games on young actresses.

"While we lived in the hotel at the same time, he was most considerate of me. I remember one morning I called the garage to bring my car around to take me to the studio, and they responded that they had other orders and could not do it. I was most annoyed, so they told me to come to the front entrance to find out why. I flew downstairs, and there waiting at the door was a magnificent limousine with a chauffeur. It was, I was told, a gift from Mr. Bern. I was most appreciative, but I told him I couldn't accept it.

"One evening I met him while waiting for the elevator. He was with a young woman to whom he introduced me, then sent her away for a few minutes on some pretext. He asked what did I think of her...that they were grooming her to become a star. I wish I could remember my answer, because the young woman was Joan Crawford."

Joan recalled the meeting. "I was under contract to MGM...playing bit parts and posing for publicity photos...meanwhile dancing up a storm at night. The studio thought me a crazy kid who got into jams because I was interested in nothing but pleasure.

But not Paul Bern. He took me to dinner many times...counseling me and telling me to take my contract more seriously. He told me, 'Improve yourself my dear. Study, work, and have patience and faith in yourself.' He was also most generous. One evening he invited Corinne Griffith and me to the Grove. While Corinne was dancing, I touched her beautiful white ermine wrap resting on her chair. It was the most luxurious garment I had ever seen. Paul asked if I liked it. Liked it? I loved it. I couldn't take my hands off of it.

"Paul left the table for a while, and later when the evening had come to an end and we left the Grove, we paused at the check stand, and instead of my cloth coat, I was handed a coat of ermine.

"Paul had had the manager of the fur shop open it up...and he bought me that coat!

"I valued Paul's friendship and he became the keeper of my dreams. His impeccable taste guided me as it guided so many others. His tragic death robbed everyone in the industry of a genuine friend. It especially robbed the newcomers, for Paul was a script searcher, talent finder, anchor and trouble-shooter."

Remembering that fatal day, Casey the doorman had been surprised to see Mr. Bern alight from his car with a flashy, pretty young actress on his arm. "Especially," thought Casey, "when he is married to the greatest dish in Hollywood."

The couple made their way to Bungalow Suite 9A, where soon they ordered food and liquid refreshments from room service. This time it was the waiter who was shocked to see the guest was Mr. Bern to whom he had served a wedding breakfast with Jean Harlow only a few months earlier.

Late that afternoon, Bern left the hotel alone, and it was not revealed until later that the episode was not his affair flagrante...rather that he had "bearded" for a producer whose clandestiness was necessitated by a suspicious wife.

Bern and the producer had actually transacted some business between themselves during the afternoon regarding a film that they were working on...and agreed that they would continue early the next morning. The producer was to come directly from the hotel to Bern's home where they would continue their work together.

When he arrived, he was met, not by Bern, but by an army of reporters and photographers. He was just in time to see the ambulance drive off with the body of Paul Bern.

Could it be, the Ambassador observers wondered, that Paul's proximity to the reckless and clandestine sex of his friend had inspired him to make love to his gorgeous bride on what was to become the last night of his life and that perhaps his mind had been willing, but his body not so?

Which somewhat explains the mystery of the manner in which Paul Bern spent the last day of his life.

Happier times . . . Jean Harlow cutting her wedding cake with MGM "wonder-boy" Irving Thalberg, his wife, actress Norma Shearer and new bridegroom, Paul Bern looking on . . . but tragedy was waiting in the wings.

Resident Howard Hughes . . . at work and at play filming his famous HELL'S ANGELS and with his star Jean Harlow.

Long-long time residents. For nine months the jurors hearing the infamous Manson trial were sequestered under 24 hour surveillance, so as not to be influenced by unrelated persons and news media. They were happy to be at the Ambassador with its gardens, pool and grounds. Even then, to visit the pool, beauty parlor or shops, they had to be accompanied by deputies. Deputies on guard. The jury on their way to court with police car escort and window-shade-drawn bus.

The "King of Swing" Benny Goodman tells a hotel story that happened to him in an old-fashioned eastern seaboard hotel where he and his band were appearing. "It was late and I was tired after a session one night, so I packed up my clarinet and headed for my room and bed. Some time later, I was awakened by a loud, urgent knocking at the door. I asked who was there, and the man answered he was the house detective. 'What do you want?'. He shouted, 'Get up and answer this door. You left the dining room without paying your check.' 'What check' I asked... 'I work here.' This dialogue went on back and forth between us for some time with him insisting I pay the damn check. Finally, I got up and answered the door. There was no one there. I stepped out in the hall, and there he was...three doors down...still trying to get in that room. We both broke up laughing when we realized we had been communicating through a transom."

The hotel had a difficult time quieting Jack Dempsey during an argument he had in the lobby with Estelle Taylor. The heavyweight champion? Nobody wanted to tangle with him. He followed Miss Taylor to her bungalow. She had quickly locked both doors...but that didn't deter him, he broke one down, crushed through the splinters, picked her up and threw her out of the window. Fortunately it was the first floor, and she landed on the soft grass. Meanwhile, the brilliant scientist Albert Einstein was next door preparing for bed and opened his door to see what was causing the racket. Debonair Jack walked over to him saying, "I've always wanted to meet you." To which it is reported Professor Einstein responded, "Thank you, but what a way to get my attention!"

It would be impossible to estimate how many weddings and receptions have been held at the Ambassador. Shown here in the East Gardens are Mae Murray and her bridegroom Prince David Mdivani with their Maid of Honor Pola Negri, and the host for their reception Rudolph Valentino who lived at the hotel at the time. The wedding had taken place at the Church of the Good Shepherd in Beverly Hills. Valentino's funeral was to follow in the same church a scant few months later.

"Call it fatalism, but from our very first meeting I knew that, somehow, this man had the power either to destroy my life or to so irrevocably alter its course that it would never again be the same," said Pola Negri the exotic beauty who had met and fallen in love with the sex symbol, the "sheik" of the roaring twenties, Rudolph Valentino.

Following Valentino's divorce from Natacha Rambova, he and Pola were inseparable, with her informing the news media frequently that they would marry. Pola was soon to lose her love as he was to die mysteriously a year later while appearing in the East. Pola was in residence at the Ambassador at the time. When the news arrived, there was an army of newsmen waiting for her to leave on her sorrowful journey to attend the wake in New York.

The bungalow door opened slowly. Newsmen and photographers rushed past security as the grieving star emerged. Fully dressed from head to toe in heavy stark black mourning veils, she paused while they asked questions and flashed photos. The crowd was so dense that some were not in strategic positions to get their shots. Pola was leaving down the garden path when she heard shouts of the newsmen to go back through the door and emerge again for their "saddened actress departs for lover's funeral" photos. And she did. That's show biz.

## Sex, Mystery and Comedy

Hotel doors open to reveal many secrets, mysteries and sometimes exposures.

Exposures? Actress Tallulah Bankhead earned a reputation for bizarre behavior, poking fun at life and enjoying every minute of it. Crazily infatuated with John Barrymore, she would crane her neck to watch his every move in the dining room, even going so far one evening as to put out her foot to trip the suave and elegant actor. Catching himself from falling by grabbing her chair, she was pitched to the floor. Talu's reward was a courtly bow, as he walked away while *she* scrambled to get up.

Later in the evening after a few glasses of illegal gin and dares by friends...Talu bribed a desk clerk to let her have a key to Barrymore's suite. When he arrived after an evening of cavorting with crony W.C. Fields in the Grove, he pulled away the bedcovers to reveal the anxious actress. Ripping off his clothes and plopping on the sofa, Barrymore told her "Another time, Talu...I'm too drunk, and you're too awkward."

An older, and even more daring Tallulah loved to shock people. Again, while staying at the Ambassador a bellman delivered a telegram to her door...to be greeted by a totally nude Tallulah. Noting the young man's shocked expression, she remarked, "Sorry, I don't have a tip on me," and swung the door shut.

★★★

As with bellmen, legion are the circumstances and stories that emanate from housekeeping. Sophie who tidies my office tells of her and another maid endeavoring to get into a bungalow suite to clean. For several days, the "do not disturb" sign was hanging on the doorknob. Finally, one morning the door was slightly ajar, and they peeked in and asked if they could enter and make the beds. They were invited in by a most hospitable gentleman who insisted they sit down and have some refreshments. Declining, he detained them showing them his wife's clothes and jewelry...and caressing her face and figure and discussing with them her dubious "charms." Escaping as quickly as they could, they reported the episode to security who upon investigating the strange goings-on took action. The next day, two men in white coats came to pick up their charges who had escaped from a local sanitarium, meanwhile the couple had found a neat spot in which to hide. With all comforts...including room service.

Screams in the night awakened the entire second floor when a honeymoon couple argued themselves into a fever pitch ending with the bridegroom throwing himself out of the window of their suite. With hysterical bride watching, he had to pick his chagrined self up from the balcony a mere three inches lower than his room. Such a night.

* * *

Jumping out of windows is not uncommon in hotel life...shattering managers because of the bad publicity. Fortunately the Ambassador has escaped this hex, but jump people will. There was an incident of a Japanese tourist throwing himself down a flight of stairs. "Severe cultural shock because of his first trip out of his own country", his tour guides called it. Again, no harm done...simply one displaced and thoroughly embarrassed person.

✶✶✶

Even more embarrassed was the Oriental gentleman who had met a young lady who negotiated to "entertain" him and several of his friends. She undoubtedly did a good job because they were all satisfied, mellowed and enough intoxicated to fall into a deep sleep from which they awakened...completely wiped out, rolled and broke.

And not a little uncomfortable was the hotel's chief of security when in effecting a search for the girl with the Rampart Division of the LAPD, the only identifying photos he could supply were polaroids of her in extremely compromising positions with the "boys".

Nude of course.

★★★

Confined to his room most of the time was a long time resident, where, it was believed, he harbored a fortune in cash. Or else why wouldn't he come out at least for meals, which after a good long time he finally did. The man was found to be charming and carefree, a total turn around of his former self. When he did retire to his quarters, it was to assiduously pore over his bible, morning, noon and night.

One morning at the usual time for his room make-up, he did not answer the maid's knock. Using her key, she entered. He had expired during the night, lying in his bed in what would seem to be the way a spiritual man would wish to leave this world. With his bible in his hands.

His family, the hotel, his lawyers and the police searched the room for the fortune that they knew must be hidden there...to no avail. It was not until months later that a maid found a fortune of half a million dollars in rare stamps pasted in the hotel Gideon Bible which in an orderly fashion, had been placed back in the bedside table drawer...and obviously unread by succeeding guests.

Three young men arrived well after midnight, weary and exhausted after a hard grinding 30-hour truck ride. They were auctioneers of Oriental Rugs and other valuable and antique items whose ventures took them across the United States. Always holding auctions and staying at the Ambassador when in Los Angeles, they however had not made a reservation for room accommodations. And there was only one room available. The clerk said he would send up a folding cot, and when it arrived, the three tired fellows, 6'3" Mike Hull, 6'4" Brian O'Conner and 6'2" Jim Burk (my son) drew straws to determine who would sleep where. Naturally, the tallest, Brian drew the cot.

Amused by the sight of several inches of Brian overhanging his bed...his companions rolled the sleeping lad out into the hallway, down and on to the elevator, and punched the button for the first floor, which opens to face the lobby exit of the Cocoanut Grove. Revelers waiting for the elevator were treated to the sight of an un-pajammaed, rousing Brian, who was as shocked as were they. Funny? Funnier yet was the fact that Brian had no idea what his room number was. You get the picture.

Jim Bacon syndicates Hollywood, is an actor and author...cohort and confidante of the stars. In HOLLYWOOD IS A FOUR LETTER TOWN he wrote about the Photoplay Awards at the Grove:

"Marilyn, late as always, just got there in time to hear her name called by Dean Martin and Jerry Lewis, who were at their zaniest in those presplit days. When she wiggled through the audience to come up on the podium, her derriere looked like two puppies fighting under a silk sheet. Her dress was so tight that it must have been sprayed on...and nothing underneath, not even panties. It was low cut, and her famous breasts undulated. Martin and Lewis went crazy. So did the audience...but there were many dissenters.

"The next day Joan Crawford, a star of the Golden Era, gave out a blistering interview to the wire services calling Marilyn's appearance a disgrace to the industry. In later years, such a blast from someone of Joan's stature would kill off the career of a Jayne Mansfield, but it only made Marilyn more colorful. Once again she had triumphed over righteous indignation.

"Nothing was ever going to stop Marilyn Monroe. She lost all her insecurities when she was flaunting that magnificent body. She lost Norma Jean Baker when she was exuding sex. A real Jekyll and Hyde complex.

"I walked out of the hotel with her. As we came down the driveway, Joe Di Maggio was outside waiting for her. 'You know Joe', she said 'He hates crowds.' "

# Lindbergh and Chaplin

Los Angeles' Herald Examiner star reporter Al Stump tells this story.

"As a taxicab pulled up to the Ambassador Hotel's entrance on a 1927 morning, two men emerged from the portico.

"One was Col. Charles Lindbergh, hero of all America; the other was Charles Chaplin, king of the movies.

"Which one should the driver take? Neither, as it turned out. A donnybrook broke out among the many taxi drivers awaiting fares, punches were thrown and bodies hit the cement.

"Yells rent the air as the rivals fought to carry off Lindy and Charlie...but as history tells it, Lindbergh departed in a hastily summoned limousine and Chaplin ducked back into the hotel...probably for a drink to quiet his nerves."

* * *

Why were guards standing in front of each of the public rooms? Sales had booked a convention...by an innocent enough name...the participants appeared usual looking, nothing out of the ordinary. But why all the stealth and mystery? Waiters were not allowed in to serve, and padlocks shut the rooms up tight each night.

Soon, hotel personnel...with their built-in radar, drums, grapevine or whatever it is that unearths information knew what was going on.

And soon, so did the local press!

It was the film festival...where films are shown to theatre owners for purchase and showing...all pornographic. Equally as weird and wild...so the grapevine had it, was the presentation and service by shapely (and uniquely clad and unclad) purveyors. Thus, the guards and padlocks, etc.

JAMES BACON

# A House Warning

You want to hear a real horror story about the high cost of Beverly Hills real estate?

Had dinner the other night with Tony Quinn at Hall and Lupita Bartlett's house in Bel Air.

Tony has been living in Rome for the past several years but thought he might look for a house in Beverly Hills. He's in town now for a special showing, for Oscar eligibility, of Bartlett's "Children of Sanchez."

"The real estate agent took me to a nice house on Bedford Drive and said the asking price was $1.5 million," said Tony.

"It was the same house I bought from the singer, Gladys Swarthout, in 1942 for $25,000. I sold it to Greta Garbo for $35,000 when I went in the army," said Tony, who may stay in Rome after that shocker.

There's a happy punchline to that story. Tony and Garbo became great friends. She admired his taste in art.

"One day we went down to the Hatfield galleries in the Ambassador Hotel. She bought six Renoirs. On the way home she said, 'Oh, Tony, I shouldn't have bought all those Renoirs. I insist we go back and let you buy one yourself.' Well, in those days I didn't have $20,000 a Renoir cost but no actor would ever admit that. It took me seven years to pay it off but I still own a Renoir."

Tony now could probably trade that Renoir even for that house in Beverly Hills he used to live in.

# "Say It Isn't So"—Columnists, Publicists...The Players And Their Games.

"There is no denying that Hollywood's fabled tycoons began as furriers, pitchmen, junk dealers, and ne'er-do-wells, but in the end they proved themselves showmen. They recognized the potential and created those early nickels and dimes into big business...major studios", said George Eells in his book, about how it all began. "And from these studios came masses of kitsch, quantities of light entertainment and at least a few genuine works of cinematic art."

Little did Thomas Alva Edison, prolific inventor and movie pioneer, and his friend George Eastman, from whose Rochester, New York laboratories came the first effective roll film, know to what lengths their inventions would travel, nor that they had inadvertently created one of the world's largest and most influential, wealthy industries.

And from the primitive series of moving pictures that extracted nickels and dimes from unsophisticated audiences did rise the spectacular motion picture art and science which so greatly has permeated, influenced, amused and sometimes bewildered the world.

As the motion picture business thrived, so did peripheral businesses. Ultimately big business also moved into the area. A natural evolvement was press coverage.

The power of the press became more evident in Hollywoodland as the film industry grew; as national radio, then television broadcasting settled in; and as international businesses and the aircraft industry burgeoned...bringing with it the need for foreign as well as domestic coverage, electronic and print, and writers of every beat from hard news to dining, entertainment to politics and everything in between.

Seeds of new business, industry, entertainment, sports...any new game in town...were planted and nurtured by the clientele who frequented the Ambassador, or who made it their headquarters. For instance, when Sam Goldwyn moved his studio to Culver City, took into his organization the financial interests of Du Pont, Chase National Bank and the Central Union Trust Company while he was still headquartered in New York, he retained a permanent suite in the hotel in order to oversee his West Coast activity.

William Randolph Hearst ran his national newspaper dynasty from a wing of the hotel...meanwhile creating plans and acquiring works of art for his own castle.

A young Howard Hughes, having freshly acquired his father's tool company was busily planning other acquisitions and starting his own film studio, meanwhile majoring in golf, flying and girls. All from his second floor suite.

Without the legendary gossip columns and chroniclers of the activity of the movie stars both on and off the screen...and the reporting of movie productions and stories of the studios and moguls, "Hollywood" may never have gotten off the ground. Stories of beautiful people, excitement, and the glamour that movie-making generated poured out of early Hollywood and was a panacea to a war-weary, dreary, mundane world.

As the columnists developed to report Hollywood, so too was the need for "publicists"...probably the earliest development of this profession...to dish out or conceal the shenanigans of the business.

Rising in importance to the industry in keeping balance, control and order, while releasing the "news" were publicists Howard Dietz, Harry Brand, Howard Strickling, and Perry Lieber, among others, hired to represent, promote and protect studios and stars. And Cohns, Zanucks, Mayers, Goldwyns, Thalbergs, Selznicks, Scharys, Schenks, Zukors, Yates, DeMilles, Foxes, Warners, Goetzs, Skouras', Laemmles and Laskys...the tycoons of filmdom.

Thus the columnists and publicists became the communicators, the conscience and the soul of the movie business...the eyes and ears that allowed for everyone "out there" to vicariously feel a part of the rich, exciting and absurd Hollywood life-style.

At one time more than 400 accredited newspaper and fan magazine correspondents covered Hollywood hijinks, to be telegraphed to people hungry for a little color and vicarious fun in their own lives.

And over the years, not the least of these were Sidney Skolsky, Army Archerd, Sheilah Graham, Hank Grant, May Mann, Jimmy Fidler, Jimmy Starr, Florabel Muir, Dorothy Manners, Rona Barrett, Marilyn Beck, Radie Harris, Jim Bacon and Joyce Haber. Their names, activities and fame became nearly as renowned as the "stars" they wrote about. Consider Louella Parsons and Hedda Hopper in their heyday. The two *became* "stars" not only tantamount to those they wrote about...but so powerful as to cause careers to be accelerated or buried with a sentence. They could create a kingdom or wipe out a studio with their daily reports which circled the globe (reaching nearly a hundred million people via a couple of thousand newspapers). Parsons and Hopper were relentless in reporting Hollywood, going far beyond the responsibilities of linking the "inside" of Hollywood with the outside world, earning for themselves some friends, many collaborators and informers, and a host of enemies.

Clockwise top left: Sammy and Mrs. Davis being interviewed by another famous fellow, VARIETY's Army Archerd. Hedda Hopper sharing a scoop with Columnist Louella Parsons. Chronicler of the stars Rona Barrett receiving a morsel from comedian Milton Berle. Famous for her fabulous chapeaux, Hedda Hopper can't get hers back from Freddy Martin and Gary Cooper.

Nor did producers escape the flattering, sometimes poisonous pen of many of the columnists. And what better reason for a number of them to join in honoring Louella on the occasion of her 35th year in the newspaper business. Her competitor Hedda told about it:

"Every producer who heard about it wanted to participate. The Ambassador's Cocoanut Grove was hired and treated to a face lift for the big event. It was originally planned to collect $25 from each of the hundreds of guests who sat among the papier-mache monkeys and imitation palm trees, but when Hearst heard about it, he footed the whole bill."

Variety reported: "The guest list was the Who's Who of motion pictures, and even the oldest old timer could not recall when so many reigning stars of the past, present and future, in toto, as well as agents, press agents, producers, directors, authors, distributors, studio chiefs, maitres d'hotel, the mayor and governor all got together in one room. Flanked by industry leaders, Miss Parsons sat on a garland-strewn dais and listened to oratory in which no adjectives were spared."

Time's account noted: "Such well-established stars as Clark Gable and Cary Grant allowed themselves the liberty of not attending."

Another who didn't take the event seriously was Hearst's beloved Marion Davies. Her drinking at that time was well-known, and her entrance was noted to be unsteady. Louella's dramatic descent down the wide staircase to the accompaniment of 'Lovely to Look At', seemed to strike Marion as hilarious. Her greetings to Louella of "Hello, you old bag, you!"...with the addition of a few four letter words, were, however, not reported in Lolly's columns describing the party.

Hedda reported that she was not invited to the celebration, "nor was Adela Rogers St. Johns...Hearst's chief sob-sister reporter."

Nor was Hedda invited to Hearst's gala reception at the Ambassador for Lindbergh for his solo flight of the Atlantic. When her son Bill was crushed that he was not to see the flyer...Hedda immediately piled him into her car...drove to the hotel, and "crashed" the party.

Bill met his hero.

Hedda spared no invectives in reporting another incident. In her book she recalled: "The Clan was riding high the night Eddy Fisher opened his night-club act at the Ambassador Hotel here, before the CLEOPATRA debacle got under way. Frank Sinatra and his henchmen took over and mashed Eddie's performance. 'It was a disgusting display of ego, snorted Milton Berle, sitting in an audience that included comedians like Jerry Lewis, Danny Thomas and Red Buttons, any one of whom, if he'd wanted to, could have joined in and made the Clan look silly. Elizabeth Taylor, still on Eddie's side that night, raged: 'He may have to take it from them but I don't. One day they'll have to answer to me for this.' "

The feud between Hedda and Louella was never to abate. Hedda wrote, "Some of us San Simeon regulars discovered that Louella wasn't slow to take credit. When W.R. and Marion went abroad on one of the many voyages they made together, we decided to throw a party for them on their return. We intended it as a gesture of thanks for all the parties of theirs that we'd enjoyed. We put on a terrific evening at the Ambassador, with its rooms crammed with flowers and cockatoos, and split the bill between us; $175 apiece. Louella was one of the party, and I'll be damned if she didn't write an article for a national magazine and take credit for it."

The Ambassador was the West Coast home to Walter Winchell, "the daddy" of gossip columnists, for over 50 years.

Maurice Zolotow author of NO PEOPLE LIKE SHOW PEOPLE, was in Los Angeles interviewing "glamourous personalities for magazines." Exhausted from the "hectic rush, rush, rush of keeping up with good old Dino and his serious drinking, attending funerals and banquets with George Jessel, stalling of Marlon Brando, burning of interview notes by Jerry Lewis, broken appointments and promises, "and finally", a tiring, terrible session on the golf course with Dean Martin...the only way, Dean insisted, he could relax and speak to reporters, Zolotow was unwinding in the Beverly Hills Polo Lounge with a martini.

"I was paged. I picked up the phone and was invited to a banquet at the Ambassador where the Press Club was honoring Walter Winchell. According to Herb Stein, columnist for the Hollywood Reporter, I would do myself a lot of good, and would meet Darryl Zanuck and some real important people because Twentieth Century-Fox was laying on the party. I should have said no, because the idea of another banquet was repulsive. But I said yes.

"Winchell was sitting at the head table. There were about 80 persons present. On Winchell's left was Zanuck and on his right was a gorgeous blonde woman in a very low-cut sequin skintight gown. She had a heavy layer of makeup and long fake eyelashes and enormous vermilion-lipsticked lips. She looked like the quintessence of the studio-manufactured sex body. I had never seen her before. She looked empty inside. She was Marilyn Monroe.

"She didn't say a word. She listened to Winchell, who was a nonstop talker and talked almost entirely about himself and his deeds. After the speeches and handshakings, I had my photograph taken with Winchell and Marilyn. For one moment, our eyes made contact and I looked into her soul and glimpsed a fear and vulnerability that made me shiver. What she was inside was not what she was outside. I suddenly said to myself I will write a book about her."

And Zolotow did just that. His book on Marilyn was completed two years before her death.

**"Ol' Blue Eyes" Sinatra singing for the Press Club. The Greater Los Angeles Press Club was headquartered at the hotel for several years.**

**Walter Winchell . . . "turned on" by Marilyn Monroe.**

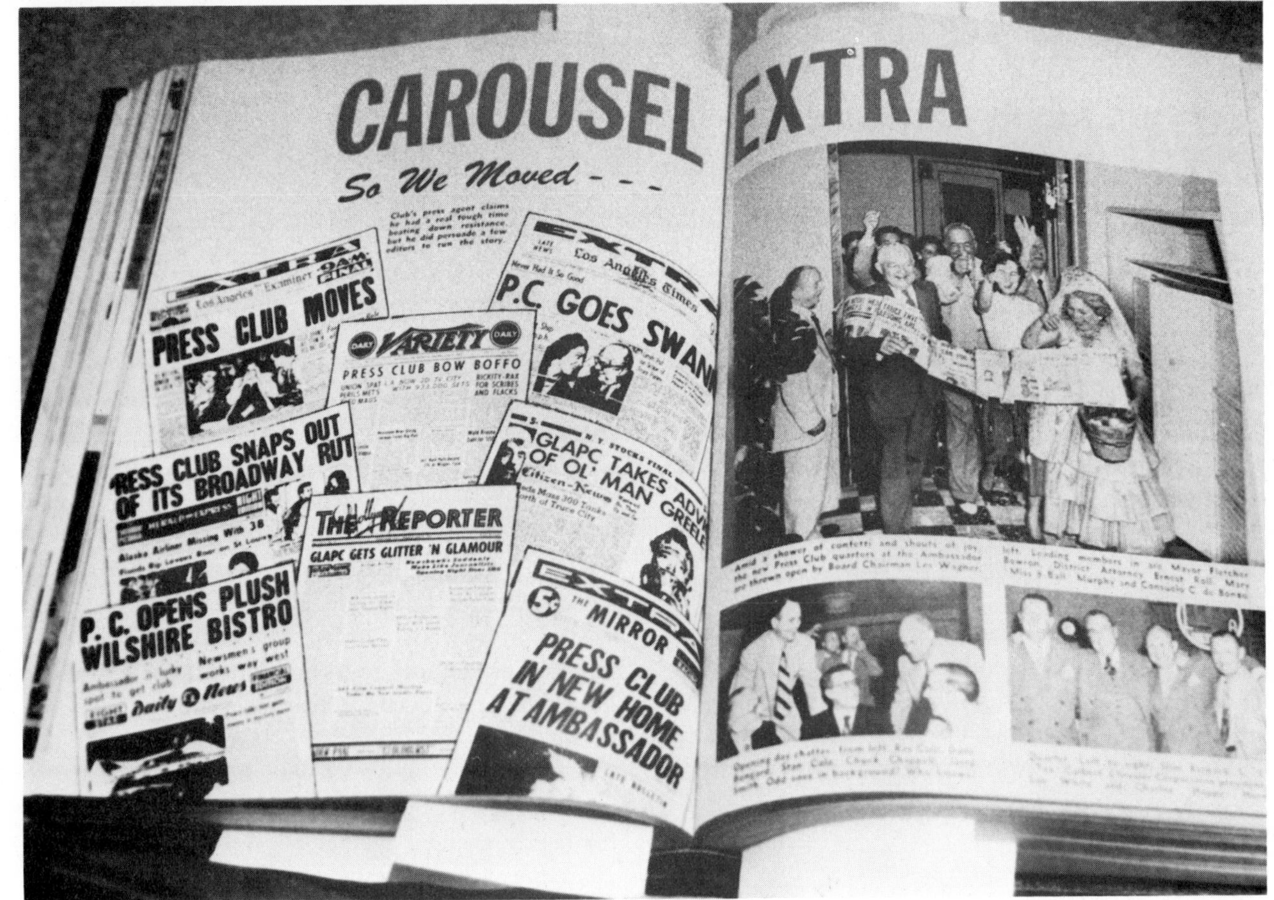


A natural home for the Greater Los Angeles Press Club, was the Ambassador where they headquartered for several years. And Marilyn was their first "MISS PRESS CLUB."

Organized in 1947, the Press Club celebrated their first anniversary with a luncheon at the Cocoanut Grove which was attended by a capacity audience of 950...the first reservations made from 15,000 requests.

The honored guest was greeted as he stepped off his special railroad car by high military and government officials; the Navy Guard of Honor; representatives of the City, County and State. They proceeded to the hotel accompanied by a parade of four marching units of 500 Army, Navy, Marine Corps and Air Force men, 100 automobiles, and hundreds of thousands of cheering fans.

Over 100 Army, Navy and Marine Corps planes dipped low over the celebrants as they moved down Wilshire Boulevard to the hotel.

In a state of shock that their invitation had been actually accepted were club members Gene Sherman, Sid Hughes, Walter Ames, Marvin Miles, Jack Cravens, etc., etc., who had extended it half jokingly.

Overnight, the Press Club, brawling, young, brash and still in swaddling clothes, had matured and become seasoned they realized...as they rode in this historical parade on June 14, 1948 with Margaret, Bess and *President Harry S. Truman* on their way to the Ambassador.

Marilyn was the first "Miss Press Club."

Unexpected guest . . . President Harry Truman.

# Liza, Hubert, Ky and Me

Late on this scene, but nonetheless vivid have been my experiences of both pain and pleasure with the news media.

A public relations expert's job is largely to attract the press by most any means short of mayhem or murder. But the reverse at times is a necessity. And to tell your friends in reportage that they cannot "cover" or be allowed into a kitchen when *again* a survey is being made of where the Kennedy death bullets lodged, for instance; or that you cannot supply a resident-John Wayne interview (and you can't divulge the reason... that he isn't wearing his hair piece); or that you've lost Frank Sinatra whose security is tighter than the Governor's; and you have some cajoling to do when political writers are trying to learn from which bungalow a campaigning President's copy and endorsements are emanating...is understandably trying. And frustrating.

A single action many times can label the PR practitioner either genius or flop.

The former I enjoyed on one occasion merely on the weight of an unpremeditated blurt, and the latter due to sheer excitement.

Of the first, a hot and heavy demonstration march was gathering momentum with dozens of shouting people carrying and wearing signs, and performing for the television, radio and newspaper crews.They were protesting the press conference for President Ky of South Vietnam taking place at the hotel.

Ky had just concluded the conference and headed for the Cocoanut Grove where he was to address the World Affairs Council. My duties with the media concluded simultaneously, so I sped out to the front lawn knowing that this conflict would create negative publicity, possibly damage, for the hotel. Reaching the protestors who were giving their dramatic all for the newsmen, their leader asked me where Ky was. I answered, "Oh he has already left by the back door." He picked up his bullhorn and shouted to everyone, "Break it up, Ky is gone." Which they did, and Ky was left to deliver his speech without further incident. Hotel management, needless to say, was relieved. My media friends were as surprised as I at how it was concluded...but smiled conspiratorily and folded up their equipment.

No hero was I the night I held up the Grove show for nearly an hour waiting for Vice President Hubert Humphrey who requested to see his "favorite performer" Liza Minelli. Liza was doing a repeat engagement at the Grove when she was just beginning to make it in the big time. Starting with a scant audience, each show would see more reservations, and on this night, the room was sold out. However, we moved people and tables around to make room ringside. The hotel manager, on hearing of the notable guest, drove all the way out to Newport Beach to fetch his vacationing wife and his tuxedo...(which required another round trip at the end of the evening to return both) to appropriately welcome the honored guest.

And no Humphrey. And no way to contact anyone, anywhere to get a clue to what was happening. I did not know the Vice President's schedule, and his local political office was closed, so could not contact him. I whipped back and forth to various entrances where I had stationed security officers...then up to the Grove again and again, to insure a proper reception.

We waited and waited. So did the audience. After dozens of announcements and just before the rapping on tables began...thankfully I received a call from Joe Cerrell, Humphrey's political representative (who was enjoying an evening elsewhere). He had gotten word of the dilemma somehow, and that his representative-in-charge had not reported back to us. The Vice-President's party had been detained...and we were to cancel the reservation.

Egg on my face? You bet...but a lesson was learned. Never, never, never hang loose in this business without someone on the other end of the answer-line.

*100 Asian-Americans in anti-Ky march*

# Good News

Variations and time requirements in my responsibilities to the hotel, happily allowed for me to enlarge the office to include an experienced, brilliant and congenial partner, Marylin Hudson, under the banner BURK/HUDSON PUBLIC RELATIONS. For the record, hotel publicity experience is invaluable inasmuch as one deals with every diversified type of event imaginable coming into and being publicized by the hotel. Therefore, our office has the need and opportunity to work with editors and news persons in many different categories. In other words, we do not specialize in any particular area, and so constantly deal with a variety of editors covering promotions and publicity in entertainment, food, personalities, religion, business, the arts of music, dancing and artists, authors, finance, ethnic groups, political, press conferences, symposiums, conventions, etc.

So one gets to know the producing, publishing and reporting greats in this business that keep the world informed about Los Angeles and suburbia.

It's impossible to mention and thank them all, but some very special people we work with are: ASSOCIATED PRESS' Bob Thomas and Ben Brown; Joe St. Amant, John Lowry, Carlos Schiebeck, Vernon Scott, Glenn Waggner and Bill Hormel of UPI; the Klines of CAPITOL NEWS, Yet Locke and the staff of CITY NEWS which serves all the news media; COPLEY and REUTERS; the Pryors, Tony Scott and Army Archerd of VARIETY; and Tichi Wilkerson Miles, Frank Barron, Hank Grant and Bob Osborne of the HOLLYWOOD REPORTER; Gil Thompson of the B'NAI B'RITH MESSENGER, one of the most respected Jewish publications in the world; KEY's George Falcon, GLENDALE NEWS Gregg Hunter, POST NEWSPAPERS Wayne Poley and MEREDITH'S Stan and Mary Roberts...and Fil Perel who covers the entertainment and restaurant scene as do Chris Barnett, Elmer Dills...and the "queen" of restaurant writers, Lois Dwan who did me an enormous favor after she politely consumed a not-so-hot dinner in a restaurant we were representing by remarking, "The best thing I can do is simply *not* to mention it in my column"; WHERE, GUEST CHECK-IN, INNKEEPER and hotel and airline magazines; Jane Gilman and Dawne Goodwin's LARCHMONT CHRONICLE which covers the social and business scene in Hancock Park and environs; Nan Dayhoff, the same for PARK LA BREA NEWS...on-camera expert reporters and commentators Regis Philbin, Stan Chambers, Nicole Pierce, Pat Li, Johnny Grant, Ben Hunter; the TIMES' Otis Chandler, Jean Sharley Taylor, Beverly Beyette,

No.1 Newsman Walter Cronkite with Ambassador Tino Mendez.

Janice Mall, Barbara Saltzman, Leonard Feather, Jack Smith, Art Seidenbaum, Jim Murray, Charles Champlin, William Wilson, Jody Jacobs, Marylou Luther, Bob Epstein, Dan Sullivan, Martin Bernheimer, Bob Hilburn, Jerry Hulse, Cathy Coyne and Harry Nelson...photographers, and Wayne Warga who took the time to write a charming letter about once living at the Ambassador when he was a child.

And the EXAMINER's Jim Bellows, Don Goodenow, Jackie Dashiell, Mary Anne Dolan, Jo Mosher, Al Stump, Mel Durslag, Norm Dash, Francis Dale, Dick Sheppard, Arelo Sederberg and Hollywood's own Jim Bacon.

Television's Ralph Story, Melody Jackson, Ruth Ashton Taylor, Bob Hilburn, Bob Banfield, George Putnam, Daniel Villanueva, Gerardo Pallares, Jess Marlow, David Horowitz, Red Humphries and Chuck Riley of KTTV whom one consults for technical and timely information; Ginny Fosdick who books *talent* for the Johnny Carson Show, and Don Kane who does the same with expert ease for Merv Griffin; the great DINAH and MIKE DOUGLAS shows; radio's inimitable Mr. Blackwell, Cecilia Pedroza, Phil Malkin, Cleve Herman, Tommy Hawkins, Michael Jackson and Paul Wallach...not to forget Toni Gilbert, Mary Jane Hewett, Skip Echols, Polly Warfield, Patte Barham, Jay Parsell, Carole Hemingway, Joy Nuell, jazz and big band preservationists Leonard Feather, Chuck Cecil and Harvey Siders...and how sorry I am I can't mention them ALL.

And, of course, everyone's friends Lohman and Barkley, with whom KFI and I wake up every morning. From "WALKING ON WILSHIRE" to a "preview" of a Rose Bowl Game (with about 100 people in that vast football arena) to judging beauty contests, they're on call and with such great humour and willingness.

Is it any wonder that the whole world is aware of Los Angeles?

# Fabulous Wilshire

"From its beginning a hundred thousand years ago as a meandering animal trail to its present status as the glamour avenue of the nation, Wilshire Boulevard has been the favorite highway for nightmarish mastodons and sabertoothed tigers, the main intervillage road for the aboriginal settlers of the region, the path followed by the first white explorers, the Camino Real of devout Catholic padres, the cattle trail of Spanish-Mexican rancheros, the brea road over which lumbering ox carts hauled brea (tar) to roof the adobe houses of the pueblo of Los Angeles, and at the turn of the century the horse and buggy picnic route to the beach," so wrote Ralph Hancock in 1949.

"Here in the longest and widest boulevard in the country are all the things that other American boulevards would like to be, plus a few things that none of them want.

"There are crowded sections of modern stores and office buildings and whole blocks of nothing more than weeds and wild oats; the country's newest and finest hotels stand cheek by jowl with smelly parking lots and rococo gas stations; there are green lawns and rows of graceful palm trees separated by jungles of brambles and the ubiquitous geranium. On this street are the most famous cafes in the world, and some of the most garish hamburger joints. And here also are the world's elite department stores...Bullock's Wilshire, I. Magnin, Saks Fifth Avenue...and all of the chain stores.

"Of all the streets in America whose names are as well known as the cities they serve, this, perhaps the oldest of them all, is a product of today and of men still living, for only its route is ancient and all its present as contemporary as today's newspaper.

"This is Main Street, Los Angeles, California! More than any other street of the surrounding sprawling 'forty suburbs in search of a city', that Los Angeles is dubbed, Wilshire sums up all of the factors that make Los Angeles the most representative city in America. To know the Boulevard intimately is to know the city and to know Los Angeles is to know a cross-section of the United States, for all of the currents and cross-currents of American life and their attendant whirlpools flow through this sunlit valley.

"Destiny, for better or worse, picked Los Angeles to do a gargantuan job. Predictions of its future are read in its contemporary statistics and its pattern of past developments, forecasts always exaggerated yet invariably fulfilled. All its elements are astonishingly large and vigorous; geographically, it is the largest city in the world; it is the lusty record of American transplanting on the roots of a Spanish-Californian culture; socially, it is made up of every class, but it is, like America, predominantly middle class; culturally, it dictates to the world though it has yet to establish fixed traditions of its own; industrially, its aptitudes are enormous and agile; politically, the electorate generally swings pendulum-like between the radically eccentric and the right of center."

Self-designated and directed, the Wilshire Chamber of Commerce since its 1920 beginning aided and abetted the building of the boulevard and the city. Not only did they expound on the beauties of their chosen area, but far and wide they extolled the virtues of abundant land and sunshine in an effort to attract national business enterprises. Today, Wilshire Boulevard boasts high rises and major companies representing insurance, banks, savings & loans, investment companies...oil interests, advertising and public relations agencies as well as the most fashionable of shops, department stores, great restaurants, parks and museums.

A few past presidents of the Wilshire Chamber of Commerce. Seated: Milan Bump, Don Hinkley, Margaret Burk, Dick Childs, Joe Houser, Ed Flam, Bill Birnie, Dick Morrell. Standing: Frank Dutra, George Allen, Al Roberts, Gordon McDonough, Joe Capalbo, and Malcolm Rutledge.

# Los Angeles Nobility

Much of Los Angeles "nobility", the first families and social elect reside in homes in areas adjacent to the Ambassador in Hancock Park, Fremont Place, Windsor Square and Larchmont, and in condominiums and apartments in the Park La Brea and Ambassador communities.

Early settlers read like a "Who's Who" of California. Designing and ruling the city were the families of Doheny, Huntington, Van Nuys, Crocker, Banning, Newmark, Van de Kamp, Janss, Duque and several of California's Governors...ancestors of many families who have remained in the area.

Still a center of culture, art and history with Mrs. Norman Chandler's (the Los Angeles Times Chandlers) neighbors aiding her in the development of the magnificent Music Center; the Windsor Square-Hancock Park Historical Society begun by Sid Adair, Jane Gilman, and Pat Hug avid in its preservation of the area; along with other groups such as the Hancock Park Art Council and the local Garden Club, and the significant Museums of Art, the community remains perhaps the most impressive and beautiful in Los Angeles. The geographical heart of the city in reality; none other is so strategically convenient to business, movie studios, leisure facilities and entertainment.

As did some of Hollywood's biggest stars live in the neighborhood in the early days including John Wayne, Nat King Cole, Jackie Coogan, Mabel Normand, Laurence Tibbett, Marian Davies, Mary Pickford, John Barrymore, Harold Lloyd, Lewis Stone, Claire Windsor, Ben Turpin, Buster Keaton, Norma Talmadge...and Mae West who is still here...and Howard Hughes when he purchased a home on the Wilshire Country Club golf course, upon moving from his apartment at the Ambassador, so now do many current film favorites and personalities reside here. To name a few: Karen Black, Muhammed Ali, David Groh, Carrie Snodgrass, Linda Ronstadt, Chris and Linda Day George, Donna Summers...and Mick Jagger!

Annual salute to the Police Department. Police Chief Darryl Gates in the foreground, with Chamber members MB, Rex Link, Frank Dutra and Joe Capalbo.

# A Royal House

Crown Prince Akihito and the Crown Princess of Japan. Ambassador Mizelle with His Majesty Mahendra Bir Bikram Shah Deva, the King of Nepal. President of Finland, Dr. Urho Kekkomen with Ambassador Harry Jenkinson. Greece's King Paul and Queen Fredricka.

Spain's King Juan Carlos and his Queen. Addis Ababa Emperor Haile Selassie with Ambassador Harry Jenkinson. Armenian Archbishop Kohren Payoyan of Lebanon. Prince Svasti and Princesses with MB.

# A Full House

First official banquet at the Ambassador . . . the 30th annual dinner of the Los Angeles Chamber of Commerce. Typical sales and business convention in Convention Center. University of Southern California Business School awards luncheon with president John Hubbard, baseball coach Rod Dedeaux, Alaska Lt. Governor "Red" Boucher and Dave Davidson, recipient of the Outstanding Achievement Award.

Comedy team Rowan and Martin . . . receiving awards in a serious moment. Reed Hixon, Director of the Gift Shows receiving a square of carpet next to the house phone which he used as his "office" during showtimes. UCLA Management, Labor and Business Program Director Mike Reilly with Peter Drucker.

# A Bizarre Party for Alice Cooper

**ALICE IN WONDERLAND**—Alice Cooper and the boys in the band perform at his coming-out party held, believe it or not, in the Venetian Room of the Amba

Sophia Loren and Jayne Mansfield.
Make up your own caption.

Old friends Elizabeth Taylor, husband Michael Wilding and Judy Garland at the premier for A STAR IS BORN.

# "Heeeeers Johnny" And Others...

Red Skelton aiding a Wilshire YMCA fund-raiser with a little member and Nader Ghermezian. Lions International welcoming their President . "Biggest stamp in the world" was the Christmas Seal painted on a billboard on the lawn.

Johnny Carson in a rare public appearance at the Cocoanut Grove. He was attending a Los Angeles' Visitors Council luncheon . . . plugging his town. Girl Scouts Steering Committee for annual Conference, aided by Ambassador Dolly Dunham and Mrs. Virginia Warren. Elegant picnic on the lawn . . . Wilshire Chamber Administrative Director George Allen with Larchmont Chronicle publishers Dawne Goodwin and Jane Gilman with Jerry Schuck. Ambassador waiter Tony Magnani pouring.

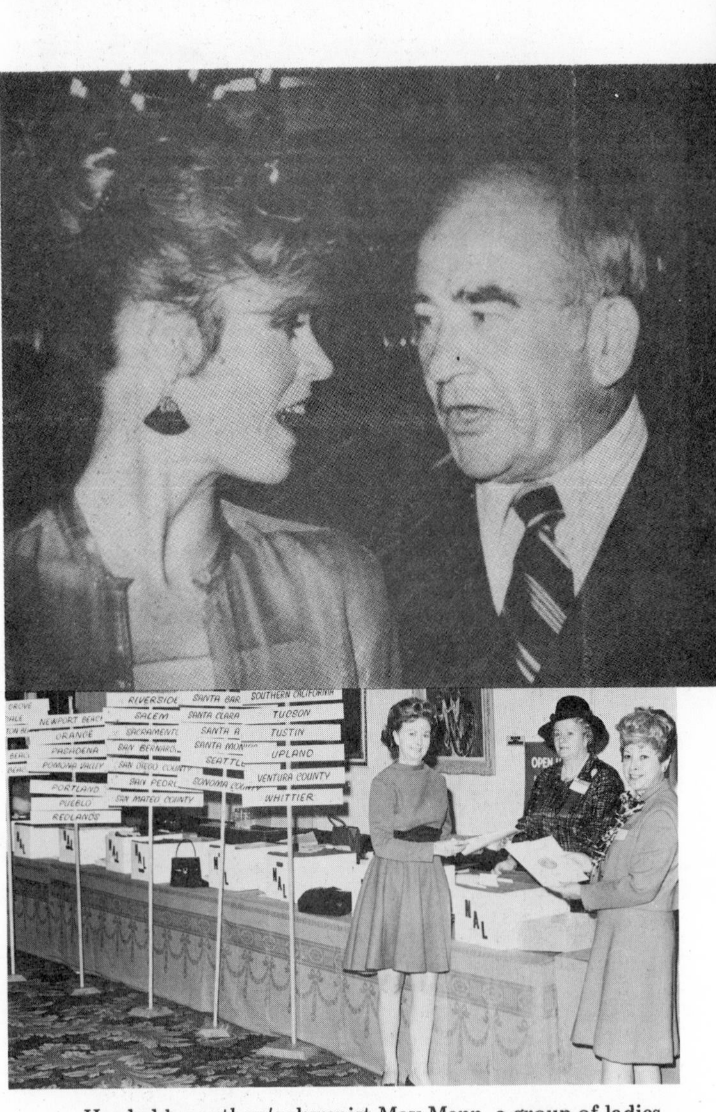

Headed by author/columnist May Mann, a group of ladies rally in support of beauty, charm and feminism . . . with the aid of famous plastic surgeon Dr. Franklin Ashley, actor Buddy Rogers and Patrick (son of John) Wayne. Supporting Bill of Rights activity: Jane Fonda and Edward Asner. Mrs. Doris Dolan, Mrs. Harry Mynatt and Mrs. Robert Fenton Craig at registration of Annual Convention of the National Assistance League.

Magnificent Headress Ball, a charity supporting event . . . showing the creativity of florist David Wittry. The greatest "thriller" of all time . . . Alfred Hitchcock, on board to address the British-American Chamber of Commerce.

Leagh Caverhill
Box 1282, Studio City
Ca. 91604 phone (213) 461-1634

★ Los Angeles Times Wed., Nov. 1, 1972—Part IV

Los Angeles Times
VIEW
PART IV WEDNESDAY, NOVEMBER 1, 1972

# Spellbinders for the Ancient Mystic Arts

406 155

BY JOHN FLEISCHMAN

Some describe her as a clairvoyant. Others say she is a psychic, a healer, a trance-medium. Leagh Caverhill calls herself a teacher of the esoteric arts, the mystic sciences that have until recently been generally discredited as a last vestige of mumbo jumbo.

But now that the Western world is courting acupuncture (the ancient Chinese medical skill) and ESP (extrasensory perception), science is having another look at parapsychological phenomena.

Meanwhile the lay public has developed a passion for anything having to do with mysticism, metaphysics and the occult. And Los Angeles, perhaps more than any U.S. city, has become the metaphysical mecca.

The reasons are complex, having partially to do with the declining influence of conventional religions and a disillusionment with the technological fruits of science.

**Answers for Living**

In the ancient mystic sciences and philosophies, people say, they find answers. And in Leagh Caverhill's classes and demonstrations, Angelenos say they have learned how to put these things to use in their lives.

Recently in the Regency Room of the Ambassador Hotel, Mrs. Caverhill hypnotically carried a young graduate student named Jeanne Taylor back through her short life, through her childhood, to the womb and then beyond into her previous incarnation as a shop assistant in turn-of-the-century San Francisco. Among those watching during the regular Thursday-night sessions were both cynics and believers.

The object of the hypnotic "regression" was to seek out the disturbance in Miss Taylor's former incarnation that caused her to react so violently to the 1971 San Fernando Valley earthquake. The reason, the clairvoyant explained, was that the young woman's death in her previous existence had been in the great San Francisco earthquake of 1906.

Mrs. Caverhill said she received this impression clairvoyantly while Miss Taylor was discussing her "irrational fear" following the February earthquake.

**Freaked Out**

"When the earthquake came I really freaked out," Miss Taylor said. "I was living alone. I didn't eat for four days. I couldn't sleep. It took me a week to get back to school. I couldn't drive under anything. None of my friends would even mention the earthquake around me."

So Mrs. Caverhill resolved to "regress" Miss Taylor to what she considered the original trauma.

The class sat quietly on the green and blue rug of the Regency Room as Miss Taylor, sitting in a straightback chair, her glasses off, was put into a deep hypnotic trance and moved back through memories of childhood and the womb.

The girl's face softened with the calm of childish sleep. Her voice became barely audible as if coming from a quiet place deep within.

"You are in a comfortable foggy place," Mrs.

Please Turn to Page 6, Col. 1

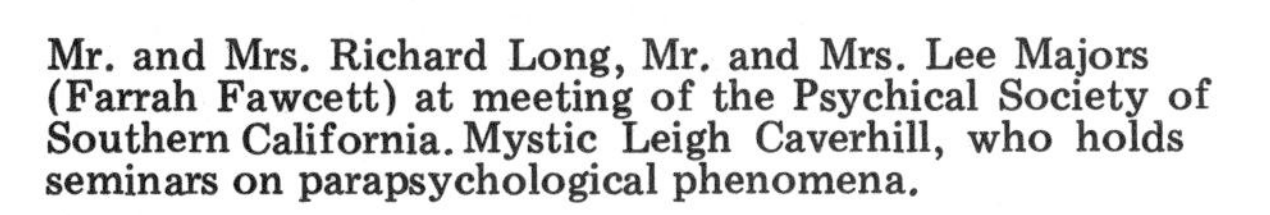

EVERY MAN A MYSTIC—Leagh Caverhill believes that everyone is endowed with psychic powers. "Each person has the answers," she says. ... doesn't need to lean on people in darkened roo

Times photo by Kathleen B

Mr. and Mrs. Richard Long, Mr. and Mrs. Lee Majors (Farrah Fawcett) at meeting of the Psychical Society of Southern California. Mystic Leigh Caverhill, who holds seminars on parapsychological phenomena.

Elizabeth Clare Prophet, Messenger for the Great White Brotherhood holding a seminar. Mrs.Prophet, "Mother" to her devotees leads a membership which numbers in the thousands. Ruth Carter Stapleton (sister of President Jimmy Carter) signing her new book. Mrs. Stapleton was negotiating to build a new spiritual facility which she heads in Texas. Los Angeles has become a metaphysical mecca, with the Ambassador, according to many religious leaders, a most conducive atmosphere for study and pursuit of truth.

(Clockwise): Nobel prize winner Linus Pauling and Mrs. Pauling. Walter Matthau plugging his and George Burns' SUNSHINE BOYS at a screening for college students. Greeting Admiral Noel Gayler, Commander of all U.S. Armed Forces in the Pacific, which encompasses over two-fifths of the earth's surface. Hosted by the Los Angeles World Affairs Council, Admiral Gayler had just returned from welcoming each individual prisoner of war released from Vietnam prisons. Beautiful little "Japanese Dolls" entertaining with song and dance. Entire family enjoying an evening in the Grove. Every Angeleno has memories of his and her special "first nights" in the famous club. Singing star Jack Jones with Ambassador Jim Miracle and his wife. Jones was relaxing after taping a national television show for Monsanto, with both his singer-father Allan Jones and actress-mother Irene Hervey at separate tables in the audience.

Clockwise from top left:

My Amy Semple McBurk. She thinks she is a staff member. May Mann and her famous "Princess" the subject of a best selling catography. Leo Rita Gross founding head of Concept Now cosmetics at her annual company party, with another four legged Leo. Protecting the lady is world-renowned couturier designer and radio/television personality Mr. Blackwell. Peggy Hamilton as bride in fashion show with many early stars. Note the little twin models. The waterfall, moon and palm trees in the background was the first seen in the Cocoanut Grove. It was to grow and grow until it was nearly wall to wall. The East Garden... ready for a wedding. Marylin Hudson receiving a peck from Robert Blake's (BARETTA) bird. And Amy again... as a young girl, in the arms of STARSKY AND HUTCH's David Soul... there are definite advantages to hotel life, Amy realizes.

Tough guy Gable doing his movie thing. Guests observe pirate scene shot with Charles Boyer, Yul Brynner and Anthony Quinn . . . would you believe . . . at the pool!

# "On Location"

Stars, producers and motion picture personnel not only live nearby, but spend an inordinate amount of working time at the Ambassador.

Guests are often astounded to walk into the middle of an action where "Policewoman" Angie Dickenson is trapping criminals in a bungalow; or to find themselves in a press conference with Sylvester Stallone in "Rocky"; to see George "Dracula" Hamilton, replete with cape and make-believe blood coming toward them; Don Meredith "Police Story" shooting an embezzler in the lobby. How about "Cannon" finding a dead man floating in the swimming pool and another "body" arriving by elevator; a "Bionic Woman" flying out of a fourth story bedroom; you'd swear you saw Howard Hughes in golfing togs, and it's Tommy Lee Jones; Jim "Rockford" Garner posing and signing autographs during his 18 hour filming day; Adam "Batman" West mincing through the lobby in wobbly heels, print dress, jewelry and batting eyelashes...in drag for a new movie image; "Wonder Woman" dueling on the roof with a movie villain; a lion lowered from the Grove ceiling in a "Magician" act. Robert Stack, Robert Wagner, or even an "Elvis" going through their paces...next day a Shaun Cassidy at the front desk with his movie "bride". Mac Davis driving up on the lawn in a $45,000 custom made car to storm into a bungalow to "save the girl"; Robert Stack controlling an entire football team, enraged by a death threat to one of their team mates. An "alcoholic" Martha Raye performing in the Grove for the "Gossip Columnist"...following a "Rich Man, Poor Man" boxing match and Gambling Casino...same place. Neil Diamond, Bobbie Vinton and Tony Bennett singing for a

More acquatic action . . . with Ross Martin and Dan Dailey.

Clockwise:
**F.I.S.T. with "Rocky" Sylvester Stallone. POLICE STORY with Tony LoBianca and Don Meredith. The Polish Prince . . . Bobby Vinton in SKAG. POLICE WOMAN . . . Angie Dickinson as Las Vegas showgirl. Lynda Carter in a rare pose...repose.**

make-believe audience and cameras in the Grove; Bob Conrad, "Starsky and Hutch", "Tenspeed and Brownshoe"... and "The Last Tycoon" all doing their things. Larry Hagman, the bad guy, in the same dining room...You know you're in "Dallas"...or you could be swimming with one of Charlie's luscious "Angels", or even sunning with "Miss Piggy". "Blind Ambition"s Richard Nixon walking down a corridor...Cybil Shepard "Guiding the Married Woman" Nancy Walker as "God", Buddy Hackett and Harvey Korman doing Abbot and Costello...a "Man With Bogart's Face", "California Fever", and Joanne Woodward with Sally Fields "Sybil" trying to separate her fourteen split selves. And of course, "The Graduate" and Fonda's "Best Man."

I book and coordinate all of this filming business, and I won't forget the young starlet in "Hooray for Hollywood" walking down the corridor to the Presidential Suite in a merry widow waist cincher...and that's all. From the front it was quite fetching...lace covering her vitals...but from the back! The garment stopped just short of the hips giving good visibility to a rounded you-know-what. I could only hope she had forgotten her wrapper. However, I would *like* to forget the filming that was booked when I was out of town. Linda Lovelace in "Lovelace for President". Sheer pandemonium and havoc...and God knows what all!

It was only a few years ago that Jayne Mansfield, killed in an automobile accident that ripped her voluptuous body in half, swivel-hipped her sensous "act" into the Cocoanut Grove, chest forward and out in a personal contest with Sophia Loren.

Today exquisitely formed Loni Anderson in a skin-tight gold lame gown plays Jayne in the same room as she is carried before the cameras dramatically on the husky shoulders of Arnold Schwarzenegger acting the part of husband Mickey Hargitay in the "Jayne Mansfield Story."

Clockwise: Robert Stack waiting for the camera to roll for MOST WANTED. Robert Wagner and Eddie Albert by their mobile dressing rooms on SWITCH location. Jack Albertson toasting Shaun Cassidy's 21st . . . while filming the SHAUN CASSIDY SPECIAL.

Just as Marilyn Monroe spent months learning to model at the Ambassador's EMMALINE SNIVELY'S BLUE BOOK MODELING AGENCY, she came back to play the "role" of model in "All About Eve", and now her life is being filmed in the Palm Bar for "Movieola."

Not to mention Lew Rawls singing for "Budweiser", and Sammy Davis extolling "Plop-plop, fiz-fiz, oh what a relief it is". Karl Maldin reminding you "Don't go anywhere without it"...and the Shasta Polar Bear and the Kellogg Tiger stalking the grounds. And Chevrolets, from antique to brand new on the East Garden lawn remind us that sometimes commercials are as exciting as the televised spaces in between.

If the Ambassador Hotel had not been identified with Hollywood by all the logical reasons of geography, personalities living in and using its facilities to entertain and be entertained...surely this relationship which has burgeoned into an additional exciting and profitable function, would have.

Dustin Hoffman, THE GRADUATE.

Kurt Russell was Elvis Presley in the film on the singer's life. It was as though Elvis was up there on the Grove stage. When the Elvis' voice wafted through the hotel . . . all the staff gathered to see and hear. That lovely perennial . . . Martha Raye starring in GOSSIP COLUMNIST. He-man Robert Conrad . . . A MAN CALLED SLOANE, and Ben Vereen in the series TENSPEED AND BROWN SHOE using the phone in MB's office.

For the hotel is, with great frequency, used as a "location" for motion picture, television and commercial filmings. Spacious grounds, enormous lobby, large high-ceilinged guest rooms, ballrooms, and especially the Cocoanut Grove, lend themselves to the needs of the film industry...costing far less than building their sets.

And so it is that guests coming to Los Angeles, often see their favorite actors and programs created before their very eyes...without having to set foot in a studio. In addition to being great publicity for the hotel, an air of excitement prevails for both guests and staff. And what could be more logical than this hotel and the film industry continuing to augment each other's efforts...as they did in this town from their beginnings.

And don't you know how much fun it is when watching your television set or visiting your favorite movie house in Tokyo or Keokuk, to point at the screen, and say, "I saw it being filmed."

The Ambassador is a "star" in her own right.

The Ambassador is often transformed into DALLAS . . .or into Washington as in BLIND AMBITION. Clockwise top left: Versatile singer/composer/actor Mac Davis studying his script for CHEAPER TO KEEP HER. Super producer-lady Renee Valente with juvenile star Stephen Collins of LOVING COUPLES. Martin Sheen, Rip Torn with John Randolph in BLIND AMBITION. Loni Anderson and Arnold Schwarzenegger as JAYNE MANSFIELD and her husband Mickey Hargitay arriving in her pink Cadillac and then into the lobby. Raymond Burr and his sidekick from PERRY MASON and IRONSIDE. Another of Renee's productions, WEDDINGS with Betty White and John Forsythe.

The Royal Barrymores . . . residents while filming RASPUTIN.

Gwen Humble, Mac Davis and Ian McShane filming on the grounds in CHEAPER TO KEEP HER.

8 IS ENOUGH on location. The "naughties" in DALLAS, Mary Francis Crosby (Bing's daughter) and "J.R." Larry Hagman (Mary Martin's son). Larry Hagman directing a segment of DALLAS.

**FLAMINGO ROAD** with new star Mark Harmon, son of movie star Elyse Knox and football great Tommy Harmon.

Clockwise top left; Richard Harris (and MB) on location. The dancingest Donald O'Conner. MY THREE SONS' Bill Demarest and Fred MacMurray. ZELDA AND SCOTT FITZGERALD played by Tuesday Weld and Jason Miller. BARNABY JONES' Buddy Ebson. ROCKFORD's Jim Garner. James Coburn one of the LOVING COUPLES.

## Very Interesting People

My worlds of exciting hotel events, personalities in the Grove, filming activity and friends in the news business, merged into a column that I began to write for the Meredith Newspaper Chain, through the support and encouragement of Walter Hicks, editors Mary and Stan Roberts, publisher Terry Donohue and restaurant/entertainment editor Fil Perel.

I was allowed a wide range of subjects in the column which I dubbed VIP...and was about Very Interesting People and Places. I have interviewed a few hundred celebrities and accomplished personalities from all walks of life, and have written about Nobel winner Dr. Linus Pauling, Pierre Costeau, Gloria Swanson, Ambassador Helm, "on location" film notables, President's wives, holidays, et al, to reminiscenses of my loving Mother...and business trips to Iran, Israel, Alaska and Japan...to the exquisitely colorful and dewy gardens outside my office window after a fresh summer rain. After seeing Adela St. Johns, this century's most famous journalist on one of her frequent television guest shots—this one on KHJ. I obtained her phone number from producer friend Gwen Howard and she became my first VIP column.

We became fast friends...and I visited Adela in various locales where the whims and/or assignments summoned this gypsy-spirit. From Malibu to San Francisco to Desert Hot Springs and the easiest...the Ambassador on one of her many sojourns...this one lasting a year.

But before she arrived to stay, Adela, Marylin and I were well into an exciting project that caught the interest and imagination of many members-to-be who joined with us in creating a literary club, which is still continuing at an informative and invigorating pace.

(Clockwise): Dyan Cannon arriving for the MUPPET PREMIERE with her daughter (Papa is Gary Grant). Miss Piggy in the arms of Charles Durning with SUPERMAN Chris Reeve waiting to cut in. Cocktails for two . . . Dick Van Dyck and "Moi" Miss Piggy. Lord Grade came from London. Producer Alan Carr with his lovely ladies came from Hollywood. A glowing Raquel Welch with her beaux she married soon after. Scintillating Ginger Rogers and sparkling Liberace.

# "Round Table Goes West"

"As in the case of the original, irreplaceable and renowned Algonquin Round Table which would never have been born except for the work of an energetic public relations proponent with a cause, Los Angeles' Round Table West...nearly 60 years later...came into being in much the same fashion," says our fact sheet.

The Algonquin luncheons were pulled together by Peter Toohey and his cause was Eugene O'Neill and the project was to get one of Eugene's, in fact his first play, produced on Broadway. An arrangement for lunch was prepared whereby O'Neill was to meet Alexander Woolcott so that he might use an item about O'Neill in his Sunday column, "Second Thoughts."

The luncheon and conversation (not too successful as far as publicizing O'Neill) launched into a long-winded dissertation of Woolcott's reminiscences of his Paris experiences and hijinks. But it got them thinking about holding another luncheon the following week for all of New York's theater journalists where they could gather together, get their attention, and hopefully develop some dialogue and topics that would be of interest to them all.

Round Table's little and very much younger sister, came into being after conversations with Adela Rogers St. Johns culminated in a keen desire to turn the American public back to the arts of reading and stimulating dialogue, between authors, would-be authors, book industry representatives, names in the news and celebrities. To enable an audience to have first

First ROUND TABLE WEST meeting (center) Joyce Haber, author of THE USERS, Carolyn See, author of MOTHERS, DAUGHTERS, and film star Jane Powell.

Adela Rogers St. Johns and Margaret.

hand union with persons whose creative and business energies are devoted to these aims, and for the latter to have a platform from which to expound their talents was our motivation.

It was June 1977 and at the time, Adela had finished the final drafts of her most recent epic, LOVE, LAUGHTER AND TEARS, MY HOLLYWOOD, and was waiting out the editing and publication in a small California desert town.

Believing that Adela...

the soft/tough sob sister, hard news journalist who had written for the Hearst Newspapers for decades; had been a story advisor to L.B. Mayer; had many short stories published, and many converted into motion pictures; had been a member of the press corps covering several U.S. Presidents; was "Mother Confessor" to Hollywood in her twenties; was a star reporter covering national and international events, crimes, trials and romances; wrote first film and star interviews and articles; created scripts; was first woman sports writer; was editor of the first movie magazine; was very influential in creating laws for woman suffrage, juvenile and prison reform, hospitals and the 18th Amendment; had her own television show; taught college classes; was a tennis champion; printed the first eye witness report on Hitler's Secret Air Force; scooped the best reporters in the world on major stories, and won the Medal of Freedom Award, the highest honor given to a civilian by the United States of America...all the while bearing, raising and supporting a family...

could better serve and be served back in the main stream of the world in a major city, we launched Round Table West.

CHRISTMAS SPECIAL . . .Paul Wallach, Adela (seated), Associated Press' Bob Thomas, Mr. and Mrs. Jesse Lasky, Jr. over from their home in London, Rod Dornsife, Marvin Werlin (seated), television's Ralph Story, Mark Werlin, author/journalist and Los Angeles Times columnist Jack Smith, and Marylin Hudson.

Marylin Hudson enthusiastically spurred the effort, and the project was launched. Cree Tante, Helen Profant, June Dyer, the Robert Campbells, "staff" photographer Richard Biegert, Alice Miller, Dawn Gregory gave their all in springboarding RTW, and Ambassador Manager Fred Gee, gave his whole hearted support.

Letters and invitations poured out to the community, and interested persons answered the call to attend the monthly meetings. In six months time, membership was in the hundreds and authors began *requesting* to be on the bill along with the famous authors and celebrities who were appearing with the inspiring and sometimes controversial Adela. Meetings have all been held at the equally Algonquin—famous west coast Ambassador.

An unexpected bonus has resulted from RTW. It has developed into a forum for current and debatable issues and causes. The audience is particularly exclusive, not by means of race, color, creed or affluency, but in the manner of interested and vital persons...concerned and caring.

RTW proved particularly rewarding to Adela personally when it became the vehicle that announced the publication and exhibit of her latest book, LOVE, LAUGHTER AND TEARS. Five days away from broken hip surgery, the author arrived at the meeting via ambulance and wheelchair on the arms of Joel McCrea and Ben Lyon to receive a standing ovation from her RTW audience, family and friends.

The Ambassador still a "star"...starring other stars, such as:

Art Seidenbaum
**Norman Cousins**
**Louis L'Amour**
**Susan Strasberg**
**Charles Higham**
**Rhonda Fleming**
**Patricia Morrison**
**Virginia Grey**
**Mrs. Jack Oakie**
**Craig Tennis**
**Art Seidenbaum**
**Rhea Kohan**
**Rudy Vallee**
**Herb Klein**
Raymond Strait
Brett Halsey
Sharon Locy
Patrick Mahony
Reuben Mamoulian
Mary Brian
Marion Nixon
Dr. Irene Kassorla
Rod Dornsife
The Werlins
Patte Barham
Jim Bacon
Diana Cary
William Dufty
John Niendorff
Dr. Omar Fareed
Robert Nathan
Anna Lee
Rosemary Edelman

John Malmin
Elaine St. Johns
Ray Bradbury
Maya Angelou
Joel McCrea
Carroll Righter
Jim Murray
Francis Dale
Robert Stack
Lilli Palmer
James Phelan
Steve Binder
Ed Haddad
Colleen Moore
Helen Rose
Dr. Thelma Moss
Chris Gugas
John Engstead
Ed Lund
Carolyn See
Gloria Swanson
Charlotte Chandler
Howard Ruff
Rosemary Edelman
Howard Strickling
Kenny Kingston
Paula Morgan
Dr. Franklin Ashley
Chris Gugas
Nathan Pritikin
Aida Grey
Charles Shows
Bob Thomas

Herb Klein
Godfrey Isaacs
Benny Goodman
Kazanjian Jewelers
Paula Morgan
Jess Stearn
Jack Smith
Ben Hunter
Kathleen Tynan
Tichi Miles
Joyce Haber
Arelo Sederberg
Joy Nuell
May Mann
Sally Presley
Ralph Bellamy
Ralph Story
Robert Young
Godfrey Isaac
Maurice Zolotow
Robert Osborn
Paul Wallach
Yvonne Fedderson
Lawrence Welk
Henry Rogers
Mary Loos
Anita Loos
Raymond Strait
David Horowitz
Jess Marlow
Marianne Alireza
Michael Crichton
Ben Lyon

Secy. of State March Fong Eu
Roy Rogers and Dale Evans

Broadcaster George Putnam . . . and his friend Adela. Colleen Moore dancing with Lawrence Welk while Adela, Peggy Hamilton and Jetta Goudal kibbitz. Economist Howard Ruff with MB and Marylin. Betty and Robert Young with Adela.

Lili Palmer, publicist Jay Allen with Anita Loos' good buddy, Gladys Tipton Turner, niece Mary Loos and early Hollywood writer Anita. Friends of Elvis Presley producer Steve Binder, Adela and Yvonne Fedderson. Roy Rogers and Dale Evans hearing it from neighbor Jane Withers. Mr. and Mrs. Robert Nathan (actress Anna Lee).

Los Angeles' leading Chinese gourmet restaurateur, elegant Madame Wu, nutrition expert Nathan Pritikin and Golden Door entrepreneur Deborah Szekely, MB and Marylin with Science Fiction's Man-of-all-centuries Ray Bradbury. Producer Gail Patrick with author Mary Loos and actresses Mary Brian and Jetta Goudal. Newspaperman Jim Bacon and Psychic Kenny Kingston.

Ambassador Hotel General Manager, Fred Gee and Mrs. Gee with Robert Stack. Secretary of the State March Fong Eu with Consumer Advocate David Horowitz. Ralph Bellamy and designer Helen Rose. Newspaper editor Jackie Dashiell with NBC's Nicole Pierce during filming of RTW for the SATURDAY SHOW.

Jess Stearn with Reuben Mamoulian signing books for fans. Art Seidenbaum with (L to R) Dody Gardiner, Georgia Soper and Dorothy Chamulon. Epicure/publisher/radio personality Paul Wallach, with Jack Smith and Ralph Story waiting to rebut. Stars' Photographer John Engstead, Elaine St. Johns, Joel McCrea, film star Marian Nixon, top MGM publicist for fifty years Howard Strickling and Ben Lyon . . . himself a film star and discoverer of sexy Marilyn Monroe and Jean Harlow.

Lawrence Welk serenading ardent RTW member Blanche Seaver with "Let Me Call You Sweetheart." The Herald Examiner Publisher Francis Dale, Adela and fans. World Affairs Council Executive Director Ed Haddad. News Anchorman Jess Marlow.

Mixed emotions. Sports columnists Jim Murray, with Hollywood Reporter publisher Tichi Wilkerson Miles

Joe Higham and Susan Strasberg

Rhonda Fleming and famed astrologer Carroll Righter.

Psychic Kenny Kingston telling it like it is to Harold Grieve and Bob Anstead.

Three great authors, Norman Cousins, Adela, Louis L'Amour . . . on the occasion of the sale of Mr. L'Amour's hundred millionth book! and the news of Cousin's book adaptation for television. Both were recipients of the RTW "Adela" Award . . . literature's answer to the Acadamy's "Oscar."

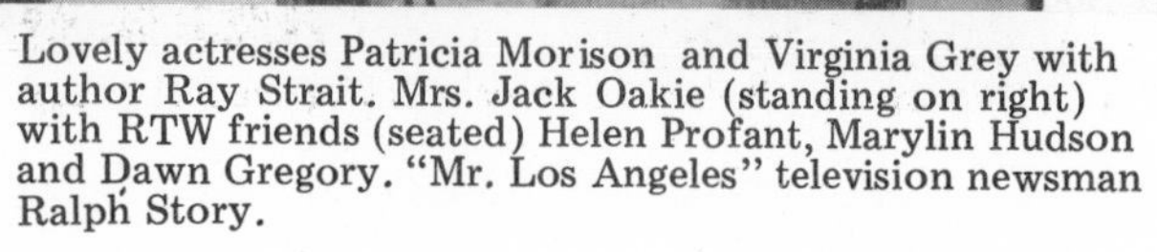

Lovely actresses Patricia Morison and Virginia Grey with author Ray Strait. Mrs. Jack Oakie (standing on right) with RTW friends (seated) Helen Profant, Marylin Hudson and Dawn Gregory. "Mr. Los Angeles" television newsman Ralph Story.

Humorist/author/columnist Jack and Mrs. Smith. Television's Ben Hunter and Mary Loos. RTW's official photographer Richard Biegert with Adela.

Dynamic and enthusiastic Maya Angelou.

Joel McCrea reading to the audience from Adela's LOVE LAUGHTER and TEARS at the meeting introducing the book.

"Leos" Jackie Dashiell, MB, Carroll Righter, Pandora Hollister, Marylin Hudson and Thelma Lager celebrating their birthdays.

# "A Night Of Nostalgia"

*You are cordially invited*
*to attend*
*A Night of Nostalgia*
*Celebrating the Golden Anniversary*
*of the*
*Ambassador Hotel and Cocoanut Grove*
*for the benefit of the*
*American Cancer Society*
*of Los Angeles*

"Florence Nightingale, Jean d'Arc and Golda Meir" was how toastmaster Georgie Jessel introduced Sybil Brand on the gala occasion of the hotel's Fiftieth Anniversary.

The celebrated Sybil is the wife of Harry Brand, equally celebrated as the original and long-time manager of publicity and stars for 20th Century Fox Studios. Georgie was referring to Sybil's association with, or founding of, untold charitable associations in Los Angeles. Her unlimited energies and resources are applied to every worthwhile cause, in fact, Harry reminds of Bob Hope's lament, "there's no disease left for me to sponsor. Sybil has taken them all." Further, her volunteer work on a county commission for innumerable years, and untiring efforts to create a suitable prison for women resulted in the Sybil Brand Institute for Women. Los Angeles County Sheriff Peter Pitchess calls her *his* warden.

"Who else to approach for a charitable cause with which to celebrate our golden anniversary," I asked myself...then Sybil, and the answer came from her on *the following day.* The American Cancer Society would sponsor the ball as their annual Los Angeles fund-raiser, to be chaired by Mrs. Wells Root, Mrs. Robert Wise (twins, who in their youth had entertained at the Grove), Henri Bollinger, Nina Anderton, Mrs. Anna Bing Arnold, Mrs. Jerry Dunphy, Mrs. Clark Gable and Mrs. Paul Schwegler.

Sybil's call went out for celebrities to appear...and again, it was "STARS NIGHT" at the Cocoanut Grove. The affair was slow to get off the ground as Cancer Chapter president, Henri Bollinger waited and waited for an answer from Grove alumnus Merv Griffin to head up the star's appearances...but when it was known that he couldn't make the date, other luminaries... friends of Sybil's, the Cancer Society and the Grove, volunteered and what a lineup! Sybil remembers it as the crowning glory of her "career". It couldn't have happened to a nicer place...or person.

"Every date I ever had when I was a single girl," Sybil remembered, "I took to the Cocoanut Grove. I went there because I had a crush on the manager's son...but my dates didn't know that."

One particular night, six young swains asked her for a date, the solution? "Let's all go together", and so she entered the Grove on the arms of six young men... their six orchids dripping from her gown, on "another of the great nights of my life."

The night? Fifty years before...*Opening Night* of the Cocoanut Grove.

Words can't express the excitement of the evening of September 11, 1971. (Nor can I. After working with the committee on all of the arrangements, illness of a relative called me to New York the night before the big celebration). So to borrow from the Times Sharon Fay Koch: *Getting misty at the Grove's 50th anniversary.*

"Jack Benny said he had his first date with his wife, Mary Livingston, and Rita Hayworth went there on her first date. Freddy Martin's medley of old Grove hits had the room misty-eyed.

"Emcee George Jessel said 'This is a very nostalgic evening. I recall coming here with my first wife...though I can't remember her name.' (Norma Talmadge, of course). Jessel introduced Mike Connors, Ida Lupino and Howard Duff, Jerry Dunphy, Edward G. Robinson, Jeanne Crain, Cesar Romero, Tippi Hedren, Jack Rourke, Mae West, Ruta Lee, Chanin Hale, Walter O'Keefe, Donna Douglas, Agnes Moorehead, the Danny Thomases, Cesar Romero, and many others.

"Jack Benny and George Burns also took their turns at the microphone. Benny borrowed a violin and played a few strains of 'Love in Bloom' ".

Columnist May Mann wrote, "Screens flashed stills of the stars who were associated with the Grove, and hundreds of stills in the foyer told their own glamourous stories. In recreating the initial formal opening of the Grove, Freddy Martin played a medley of the theme songs of all the famed orchestras who have played the room. Flowers, cocoanut palms and monkeys were again present.

"Truly one of Hollywood's unforgettable evenings. A kind of icing on the cake that has always been the great Cocoanut Grove."

"The gasps of recognition and applause as some of the famous stars arrived was worth the hundred dollar price of the ducats. Mae West was the 'Belle of the Ball'. Gorgeous with her turquoise gown, famed diamonds and long blonde hair, men flocked to her side. Many stars and performers put on their acts, but were topped with Jessel's sign-off...an Al Jolson rendition of CALIFORNIA, HERE I COME.

# Getting Misty at Grove's 50th Anniversary

BY SHARON FAY KOCH
Times Staff Writer

Jack Benny said he had his first date with his wife, Mary Livingston, there.

Actress Rita Hayworth went there on her first date.

Socialite Nina Anderton remembers attending the Sunday afternoon dances while advertising executive John D. Roche recalls that all heads turned as he escorted interior designer Leora Hamilton into the Cocoanut Grove 40 years ago.

Although today it's called the Now Grove (and emcee George Jessel, noting the modern decor which has replaced the cocoanut palms, drew applause when he said, "The Pierce Bros. have done a remarkable job"), the nightclub at the Ambassador always will be the Cocoanut Grove for generations of Southlanders for whom it was the "in setting" of the 20s, 30s and 40s.

Saturday night it was the setting for the American Cancer Society of Los Angeles benefit, and Benny, Roche and Misses Hayworth, Anderton and Hamilton joined nearly 600 guests in marking the 50th anniversary of the Grove.

Benefit chairman Sybil (Mrs. Harry) Brand, who attended not only the room's initial opening in 1921 but the first floor show the following year, re-created the opening-night menu for Saturday's benefit—fruit cocktail, consomme, filet mignon and Bombe Alexander.

Even orchestra leader Freddy Martin, who is semiretired, returned to play for dancing as well as a musical salute to orchestra leaders from Paul Whiteman to Glenn Miller who have played at the Grove over the years.

Martin, who reassembled several members of his original orchestra for the benefit (he first opened at the Grove, he said, in 1935), told the audience at the conclusion of his musical program, "I hope that we made all of you feel many years younger.

Martin also recalled that it was bandleader Whiteman, hired to play for a private party at the Grove in 1922, who gave the room its name.

"The room had been filled with palm trees and monkevs (stuffed) for this particular party. And

Please Turn to Page 11, Col. 1

Clockwise:
"Hollywood's Queen" Sybil Brand with Henri Bollinger. Edward G. Robinson, George Burns. Agnes Moorehead and popular bachelor Cesar Romero. Mr. and Mrs. Danny Thomas. Socialite Nina Anderton with her friend. Anthony Quinn with his.

The enduring Mae West with a handsome escort (as usual). George Jessel with June Dyer. Bon Vivant Henry Berger with show-stopper Ann Miller.

Barbara Anderson, Mr. and Mrs. Don Calloway. LA VERNE AND SHIRLEY's Penny Marshall and her husband Rob Reiner. Mayor and Mrs. Tom Bradley.

Sybil with Rita Hayworth. Jack Benny (who called Sybil to tell her he was disappointed not to be invited to play his violin at the party . . . naturally Sybil fixed that!) with headliner Rouvan. Even the BEVERLY HILLBILLIES came . . .

Rooster Cogburn and his sidekick, Hal Wallis, stole the show at the Hollywood Foreign Press Assn.'s 27th annual Golden Globes Awards at the Cocoanut Grove.

Rooster, alias John Wayne, alias the Duke, alias the Legend, took the award for best dramatic actor for his role in "True Grit," produced by Wallis, and two standing ovations in his stride. His speeches were short: "Happiness just stepped up and greeted me," but sparked by a sense of gratitude and pride.

Wayne reminisced about the old days at the Cocoanut Grove when you could get by on $5 and a bowl of spiked punch and watch Joan Crawford win a Charleston contest while Bing Crosby crooned from the stage. Then he took the stage and presented Miss Crawford the Cecil B. DeMille Award for outstanding contributions to the entertainment field.

"She is the queen. Joan Crawford means motion pictures," he said as Miss Crawford stepped on the stage, bare-shouldered and shapely.

WINNERS — The Hollywood Foreign Press Association held its annual Golden Globe awards at the Ambassador Hotel Monday night. Here actor John Wayne presents the Cecil B. De Mille Award to Joan Crawford. Wayne won the Best Motion Picture Actor Award for his part in the movie, "True Grit," which didn't surprise many members of the press.

Joan was snapped out of her reverie by Wayne's appearance and remarks on stage. She had been mentally counting the times she had stepped on this very stage to receive awards...from Charleston and Black Bottom contests, to Academy and Golden Globe Awards...and all the awards to others that she had applauded in between — tonight for World Film Favorite actor Steve McQueen and actress Barbra Streisand. For Goldie Hawn, Genevieve Bujold and Peter O'Toole...then most promising newcomers Ali MacGraw and Jon Voight.

She wept when Rod McKuen read his impromptu poetry scribbled "Thoughts" on a napkin, and laughed when Lee Marvin remarked to Anthony Quinn on losing to Peter O'Toole; "At least we're off the hook and don't have to make asses out of ourselves." She was pleased when Gig Young was "bowled over" by winning for "They Shoot Horses, Don't They?", and heartily applauded Carol Burnett's wit and stage presence and the recognition and awards given Patty Duke and Robert Young's "Marcus Welby".

We can't get into another's head...but was she remembering the night she had had to be dragged out of the arms and embrace of Clark Gable when he was making mad love to her behind the band shell...when L.B. Mayer saw her returning and aware of their deep attraction for each other shipped her and husband Douglas Fairbanks, Jr. to England with orders for her and Gable to "knock it off" if they wanted to protect their careers. Or of earlier days when a lover disengaged himself from this life when she spurned his love...here in this very Cocoanut Grove.

Now that it was in back of her, was she amused to remember that her beaus at Saturday tea dansants had turned from her to admire the newest and youngest member of their girl-pack, Loretta Young. Or was she remembering the thrill of the luxurious ermine coat that Paul Bern had waiting for her in the cloak room as a "little surprise" after an evening of dining and dancing. Or did she smile at remembering her frustration with Howard Hughes who would just sit alone at a table in the back of the room apparently not noticing her.

Even tonight, she was shaken upon entering the Cocoanut Grove to find intruders occupying her reserved table. Inwardly furious, she waited until John Wayne's intervention shot the intruders up and away.

Then...with Wayne's words, "She is the queen, Joan Crawford", Joan stood up and amidst the applause of the entire room walked toward him to receive another award.

As she passed she touched my arm and whispered "What memories I have of this place. Someone should write a book about it."

My favorite photo . . .
with the King of Swing, Benny Goodman.

# *EPILOGUE*

*There's so much more to "Stars" story. Much had to be sacrified in the interest of time and space...intimate and lengthy personal stories of Hollywood stars and industrialists, royalty and the rich which had to be held back. Often their stories, as they, merge to tell secrets that only the walls of this hotel have witnessed. And enthusiastic aficionados still are volunteering vignettes and information. I hope it continues...because therein lies another book. And it's on its way!*

# ABOUT THE AUTHOR

*Born in Savannah, Georgia, attended school and Northwestern University in Chicago, then migrated to California. Married to Harry Burk and Mother of Tray, Linda and Jimmy, Mother in law to Marie, Jose and Lyn; Grandmother to J.T., Jeffrey, Andres, Trevor, Alicia, and another happily expected.*

*Associated with the Ambassador since 1968, and partner to Burk/Hudson Public Relations. Columnist for Meredith Publications and freelance. Lecturer to various colleges and club groups.*

*Many civic and community affiliations include: Co-founder of Hancock Park Art Council, Founder of Huntington Organ Society, Executive Chairman of 6,000 member Los Angeles Community Advisory Committee, board member of Professional Women to the Philharmonic, and Windsor Square-Hancock Park Historical*

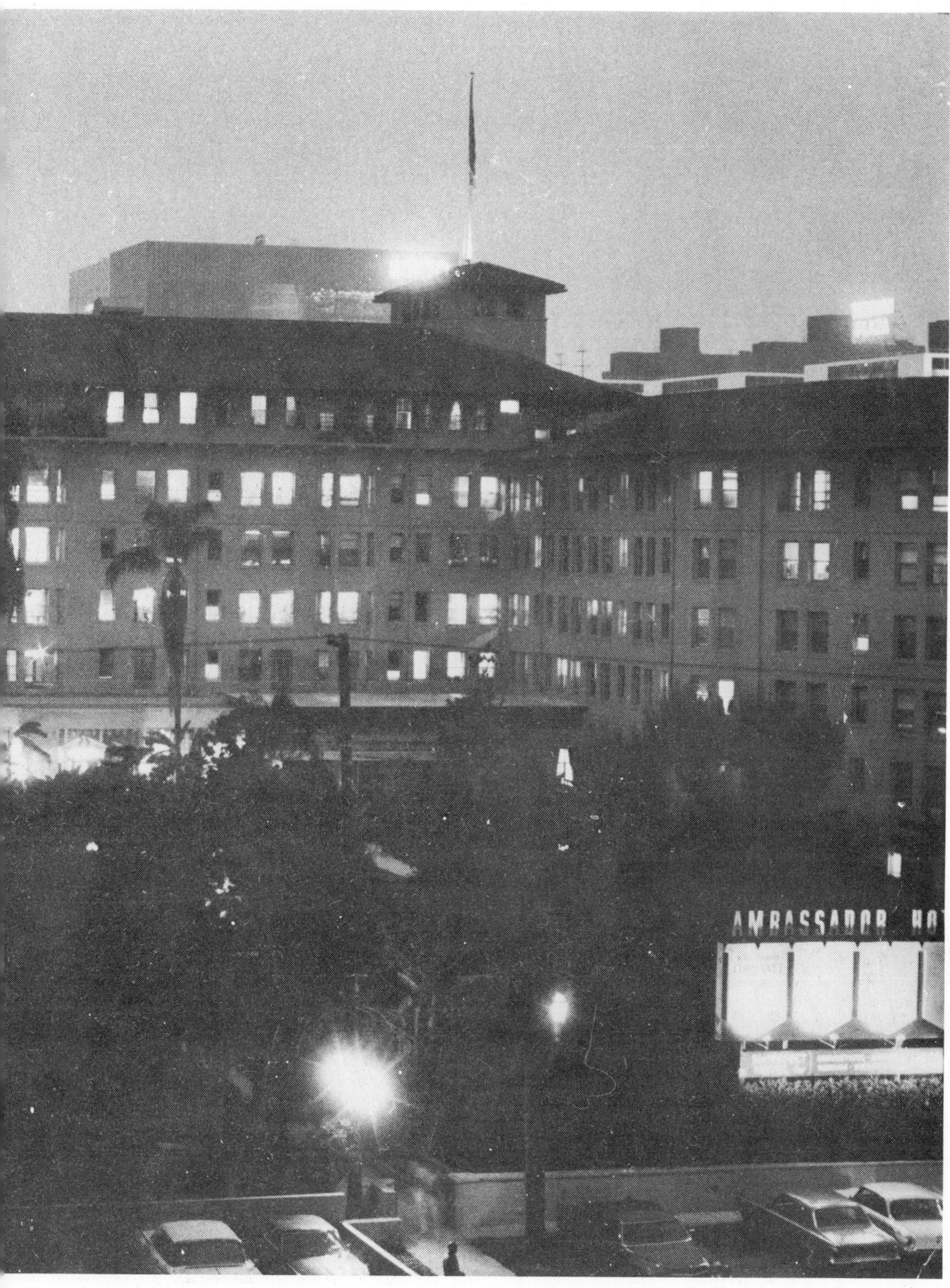


*Society, advisor to several trade groups and ethnic councils. Among "firsts...first Southern California woman named vice president of a financial institution, first woman president of Wilshire Chamber of Commerce, world's first woman member voted in to Lion's International.*

*Honors include Woman of the Year: Larchmont Chronicle and twice by inmates of Tehachapi Prison, Winner of several advertising (Lulu) awards and public relations awards (National Hotel/Motel Gold Key Award) and White House invitation for consideration of Treasurer of the United States. Prior to Ambassador activity, Mrs. Burk was familiar with hotel life as she and her husband were proprietors of the Lebec Hotel (California) She considers her most pleasant accomplishment the publication of "Are the Stars Out Tonight".*

*Long live the Ambassador and long may she make waves.*

# INDEX OF PHOTOS

# ACKNOWLEDGEMENTS

*How does one say thanks to the help one gets from one's friends? I can only hope that " Stars" , my deep gratitude and that of the Ambassador, come close.*

*Especially to my husband, for supplying so many gourmet meals and portions of patience; to "Stars" inspiration and my so-dear friend Adela Rogers St. Johns; to partner Marylin Hudson for her unrelenting nudging, concern and editing; to publisher friend Noel Dennis for her expertise, midnight oil and guidance; to George and Mary Ouzounian for their expert typesetting and tolerance of so many twelfth hour adjustments, to Linda Wexler for her detailing "Stars"; to American Offset Printers and Stauffer Bindery for the obvious; to the Tantes and Sopers for their desert oasises which without both "Stars" and I would have derailed; to Ambassador sustainers owners and managers. . . the Crowns, Schines and Gees; and to those who maintained order and provided assistance. . . Dawn Gregory, Helen Profant, Janice Mihld, Richard Biegert, Ellen Spirytus; and to all the people who treasure the Ambassador, particularly Sybil Brand, Betty and Robert Young, Benny Goodman and Robert Anstead; to Round Table West which exists to encourage books and authors; to all those who prodded with "when is that book coming out" and to my precious Mother up there who believed I could do anything, and to my kids who are surprised when I do. . . thanks, and I wish for all of you that all of your "Stars...are out tonight".*

*And oh yes, for all of you who buy the darn thing.*

To the following friends of the Ambassador who provided enthusiasm, time, information, photos, energy, research and encouragement...our gratitude.

Academy of Motion Picture
Arts and Sciences
Aherne, Brian
Aherne, Edna McNabb
Landsburg Productions
Alcaliam, Mrs. E.
Allen, Dub
Alstrom, Frances
American Broadcasting System
Anderson, Jack
Anstead, Bob
Antler, Irving
Antonio's Beauty Salon
A.P.E. Photos
Autry, Max Munn
Bach, Ira
Banks, Bill
Beatty, Loretta
Begakis, Yani
Benjamin, Carlyn Frank
Biegert, Richard
Bowen, Warren
Bracken, Denny
Bradford, Gene
Brand, Harry
Brand, Sybil
Brown, Lansing
Brush, Helen
Bull, Clarence Sinclair
Burns, Barbara
California Outdoors and In
Capitol Records
Casey, Nora
Carstens, Theodore
Chamulon, Dorothy
Cocoanut Grove Photos
Cahoon, Alice
Columbia Broadcasting System
Crane, Ralph
Crest Photography
Crown, Lester
Cummings, Roy
Cutler, Nate
Davis, Jules
de Marais, Jack
Diehl, Digby
Dollinger News Pics
Dooley, Mason
Dyer, June
Eagler, Wally
Eaton, Esther
Eltinge, George
Engstead, John
Falcon, George
Ferraro, Councilman John
Filmways
First National Studio
Fleishman, Sue
Fortier, George
Fryer, Elmer
Gage, Maude
Gaines, John
Gee, Fred
Gilman, Jane
Glendon, Pearl
Glickman, Phil
Golden, Jean
Golden, Lex
Goldfus, Sylvia
Goodman, Bennie
Goodwin, Dawne
Gray, Vesta
Greater Los Angeles Press Club
Green, Lee
Gregory, Dawn
Hallum, Lucy
Hamilton, Peggy
Hammond, Darlene
Hanauer, Don
Harvey, Bill
Herald-Examiner
Holland, Florence
Hollywood, Ken
Hollywood Nightclub Photos
Hover, Herman
Hudson, Marylin
Huff, Ray
Huntington Library
Huntley, Bob
International Graphics
Irving, Jane
Jaime, Wally
James, Umbra
Jarrett, Art
Jenkinson, Harry
JFK Space Center
Kadich, Cliff
Kelly-Rush & Associates
Kerbawy, Nick
Keystone Photos
Kleese, Frances
Kumin Tolenick Photos
Lamparski, Richard
Landman, Robert
Lasky, Betty
Lazar, Mary
Levey, Dorothy
Lorimar Productions
Los Angeles Press Club
Los Angeles Public Libraries
Los Angeles Times
Lund, Ed
Mack, Ferris
Magnin, Rabbi Edgar
Mann, May
Marble Arch Films
Martin, Freddy
Maxmilian, Oto
McCroskey, H. Everson
McDevitt, Barney
McFadden, Lee
McGregor, Bruce
McNally, Mary
Mercurio, Conrad
McWhinnie, Zetley
Metro-Goldwyn-Mayer
Mihn, Charlie
Miller, Max
Milligan, J.C.
Milton, Don
Muppets
Neel, Maurice
Osterman, R.K.
Palmer, Goldy
Paramount Pictures
Parker, Maynard
Pellison & Field
Pfeifer, Betty
Pictorial California
Plunkett, Bob
Pontrelli Photos
Profant, Helen
Rashall, Dan
Regal Productions
Reicher, Arthur
Reigl, Hans
Rifkind, Emilie Michel
Rogers, Buddy
Rothschild Photos
Sadowsky, Frances
Saliba, Dolores
Samuelson, Chief
Saunders, Claire
Schine, Myer
Schine, Mrs. Myer
Schmidt, George Reaves
Scott, Mrs. K.W.
Scully, C. Yardley
Seaman, Marguerite
Sheedy & Long
Sinay, Hershel
Skeith Photo
Skinner, Mrs. Fred
Smith, Dorothy
Smith, Jack
Soper, Georgia
Spelling-Goldberg Productions
Spirytus, Ellen
Strickling, Howard
St. Johns, Elaine
Studley, Allan
Swanson, Gloria
Swanson, H.N.
Thomas, Bob
Time-Life Productions
Title Insurance
Tozzi, August
20th Century Fox
Universal Studios
U.P.I.
Valente, Renee
Vallee, Rudy
Veedana, Kevin
Waggner, Glenn
Waits, Bob
Walker, Leo
Walt Disney Studios
Warga, Wayne
Warner Brothers
Watson, Bill
Wayne, John
Weber, Arnold
Weissman Photos
Welds, Mike
Whittington, Dick
Wiley, Hugh
Wilson, Jan Meier
Wilson, Dr. Kent
Winston, Laura
Withers, Jane
Wolf, Marguerite
World Affairs Council
Yorty, Mayor Sam
Zaharis, Pete
Zittler, Edith

NORMAN VINCENT PEALE
NELSON A. ROCKEFELLER
CHARLES A. LINDBERGH
JACK DEMPSEY
TED LEWIS
BARNEY OLDFIELD
BARRY GOLDWATER
SID GRAUMAN

ROBERT NATHAN
J. EDGAR HOOVER
TEXAS GUINAN
ELEANOR ROOSEVELT
FAITH BALDWIN
ADMIRAL RICHARD BYRD
IRVING BERLIN
WALTER WINCHELL